BEER

COCKTAILS

BEER

THE ESSENTIAL GUIDE

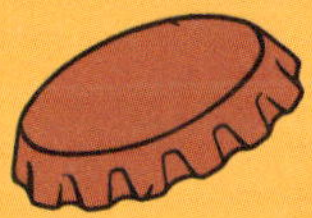

A NEW SPIN ON YOUR FAVORITE CLASSICS

CYRIL HUBERT
BEER EXPERT · BEER SOMMELIER

COCKTAILS

GELDING STREET PRESS

A Gelding Street Press book
An imprint of Rockpool Publishing
PO Box 252
Summer Hill
NSW 2130 Australia

geldingstreetpress.com
Follow us! @geldingstreet_press

First published under ISBN: 9782707214256 as *La bière en cocktails* © 2024 by Éditions Marie Claire – Société d'Information et de Créations (SIC)

This edition published in 2026 by Rockpool Publishing
ISBN: 9781922662422

Design and typesetting by Sara Lindberg, Rockpool Publishing
Translated by Cathlin Barrett
Translation edited by Heather Millar

Note: All information correct at time of writing.

Printed and bound in China
10 9 8 7 6 5 4 3 2 1

CONTENTS

FOREWORD **IX**

A BRIEF INTRODUCTION **1**

THE ART OF BEER MIXOLOGY 1

THE HISTORY OF MIXOLOGY **3**

THE DEVELOPMENT OF DRINKING VENUES 3

THE HISTORY OF THE COCKTAIL 9

MIXOLOGY BASICS **27**

GLASSWARE 33

ESSENTIAL INGREDIENTS 37

DECORATIVE GARNISHES BY CATEGORY 75

COCKTAIL CATEGORIES 114

THE BASICS OF COCKTAIL CREATION **121**

RULES TO FOLLOW 121

BALANCE 123

DISCOVERY AND CUSTOMIZATION 125

MAKE A COCKTAIL WITH YOUR FAVORITE BEER 126

REINVENTING A CLASSIC COCKTAIL WITH BEER 130

PREPARATION TECHNIQUES **133**

MIXING INGREDIENTS 133

FILTRATION 137

CLARIFICATION (MILK PUNCH) 138

GARNISHES 141

COCKTAIL RECIPES 155

SOUR BEER 157

WHEAT BEER AND FRUITY WHEAT BEER 214

STRONG ALE 230

SPECIALTY BEERS 242

IPA, PALE ALE, AND AMERICAN PALE ALE 254

LAGER 290

STOUTS AND PORTER 296

ACKNOWLEDGMENTS 308

INDEX OF COCKTAILS 309

ABOUT THE AUTHOR 310

FOREWORD

As someone who's written about beer, gin, and whisky, let me state the obvious: I like a good drink, and I like to help people discover good drinks. So it gets under my skin when I see people believing silly myths: "Beer is simple," "mixing cocktails is best left to bartenders wearing black suspenders or leather aprons," or "you can be a beer person or a cocktail person – not both." Cyril Hubert doesn't believe these myths, and he won't let you believe them, either.

In *Beer Cocktails*, Cyril talks about drinks with reverence and teaches you rules to follow if you don't want your cocktails to be a confusing mess, but he also encourages you to get creative and forge your own path. The end goal of this book isn't to be a know-it-all; it's to have fun and try interesting new tipples.

There are over 100 beer cocktail recipes – more than I've ever seen in one book before – but, even if you removed them, these pages would still comprise a history lesson on the world of cocktails; a masterclass in flavor pairing; and a laundry list of equipment, beer types, spirits, and garnishes that can be mixed and matched in more ways than you could ever imagine.

I don't know how you found this book. Perhaps you're a beer lover who's knee-deep in new breweries, experimental releases and traditional styles from around the globe, but cocktails are still shrouded in mystery for you. Or maybe you're familiar with the art of cocktails, and how to achieve complexity and balance through mixing, but you can't imagine how beer fits into that. However you came to be reading this, I promise: you'll be poring over Cyril's ideas and sipping these flavor combinations for a long time. And if your only experience of beer cocktails is a shot of cheap whisky followed by a bland lager, then hold on tight: your world is about to be shaken up, double-strained, and topped with beer.

Mick W.

Mick Wüst, author of *Beer Drinker's Toolkit, Gin Drinker's Toolkit* and *Whisky & Cocktails*.

A BRIEF INTRODUCTION

As a beerologist, I'm fascinated by the world of spirits, their history, production methods and variety. I'm drawn to the idea of exploring this vast universe and bringing my imagination to the fore. Creating beer cocktails is a no-brainer for me, and I think they'll be very popular soon. I hope that this book will contribute to the emergence of this movement.

This book stems from my love for life and its pleasures. I needed to experiment and push beer to its limits, to explore this world that was unknown to me at the time. I did my own experiments and numerous tests. This book is the culmination of my reflections, which I'd like to share with you.

THE ART OF BEER MIXOLOGY

The beer cocktail is an adventure in itself, offering fertile ground for creativity. It's a whole new world for drink enthusiasts.

Beer mixology blends ancestral brewing heritage with contemporary mixology techniques, offering a new and exciting way to enjoy beer.

This book explores new frontiers, taking advantage of beer's versatility to create unique recipes.

Explore the captivating world of beer mixology, where flavors harmonize in exclusive creations. There's bound to be a beer cocktail for you here.

It's time to break the rules and set off on a surprising taste adventure. So let the mixing begin!

THE HISTORY OF MIXOLOGY

THE DEVELOPMENT OF DRINKING VENUES

Cafés

For millennia, before Europe's cafés and pubs, social gathering places such as inns and taverns provided food and lodging for travelers, offering wine and spicy drinks.

The emergence of luxurious, typically French cafés as meeting places followed the arrival of the expensive beverage of the same name. The first coffee beans were brought to Marseille from Constantinople and Egypt in 1644 by the merchant Pierre de La Roque. The drink remained confined to the city for around 15 years.

Although Jean de Thévenot introduced coffee to Paris in 1659, it was in 1669 that the precious beans made their debut at the court of Louis XIV, brought by a Turkish ambassador sent by Mehmed IV. Coffee came into the king's favor, becoming an aristocratic beverage, a symbol of elegance, and a sign of high social status. The first coffee shop was opened in Marseille in 1671 by Pascal Haroukian. He then opened a second establishment in 1672 in Saint-Germain-des-Prés, Paris, followed by the famous Procope, founded by Francesco Procopio dei Coltelli in 1686.

Bourgeois places where coffee was served in refined, ornate porcelain cups were frequented by philosophers, intellectuals, and other members of high society. Prominent names such as Racine, La Fontaine, François Boucher, Voltaire, Rousseau, d'Alembert, Diderot, and La Fayette enjoyed this nectar at every social gathering.

After Paris, Lyon, and Marseille, coffee spread throughout Europe. Over time, it became popular and accessible to all social classes. However, it wasn't until around 1720 that it reached the provinces, the countryside, and the rural areas.

In the 18th century, cafés became essential meeting places, where the social aspect sometimes counted for more than the quality of the beverages served. Cafés played a central role during the Enlightenment, a period marked by the rise of new philosophical ideas advocating rationality, logic, and the rejection of old customs, superstitious beliefs, and authoritarian domination.

The café is described as a driving force behind intellectual movements, a place where enlightened minds gathered to discuss, debate, and develop innovative ideas. Cafés had a major impact on the transformation of society, rapidly becoming hubs for news and current affairs. Everyone had a say, regardless of their social status. Lively discussions covered major topics such as religion, politics, and the arts.

It was in the atmosphere of these lively places that the promotion of philosophy flourished and revolutionary ideas took shape, paving the way for the American and French revolutions. During their stay in France, American personalities such as John Paul Jones, Benjamin Franklin, and Thomas Jefferson frequented Café Procope. Jefferson is even said to have worked there on his draft of the U.S. Constitution. Like cocoa, spices, and tea, coffee would profoundly influence consumer habits in Europe.

FIERY BELLE ÉPOQUE

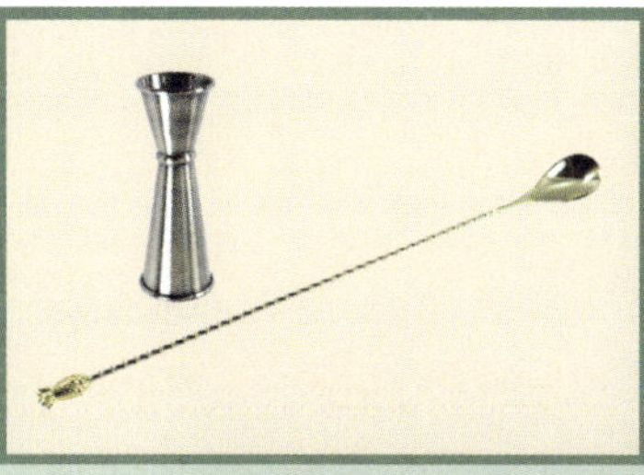

EQUIPMENT

GLASS TYPE: SAINTONGE SANDSTONE CUP

DID YOU KNOW? This drink is thought to have originated with the introduction of coffee in France in the 17th century, derives from the habit of farm workers flambéing cognac to warm cold morning coffee during lunch breaks in the vineyards.

INGREDIENTS:

- 2⅓ fl oz (70 ml) 10-generation cognac (Maison Ferrand)
- ⅔ fl oz (20 ml) Pousse Rapière
- BEER: 1⅓ fl oz (40 ml) Imperial Stout (if possible, use an Imperial Stout aged in triple sec or apricot brandy barrels)
- 1 strong cold espresso
- 1 pinch cinnamon
- 1 tbsp brown sugar

BUILD IN THE GLASS

1 – Place the brown sugar on the saucer.
2 – Pour 1 fl oz (30 ml) of cognac over the sugar and wait for it to soak in.
3 – Pour the cold coffee, beer and Pousse Rapière into the cup and stir.
4 – Pour the rest of the cognac into the cup on the back of a teaspoon to keep it on the surface.
5 – Flambé the contents of the saucer, then once the flames have died down, pour the cognac syrup into the cup and stir. Sprinkle with cinnamon.

Bars and pubs

Even older than coffee, beer, which experienced incredible growth, was at the origin of the "public house" bars and pubs as we know them today.

The specialization of beer production in England led to the proliferation of the first pubs. Such was the growth that King Edgar decreed in 965 that there should be only one pub per village. In 1393, faced with the problems regarding their location, King Richard II decreed that pubs must be identified by an external sign.

In England, Ireland, and Brittany at the time, alcoholic beverages were the main drinks consumed, as was the case in Germany, Belgium, and Italy.

However, there are also old pubs in Asia, Africa, Oceania, and America. Every culture has its own traditions of drinking and establishments where people gather to socialize.

The imperial ambitions of the British Empire often involved pubs. Today, these bars can be found in former colonies such as Australia, New Zealand, British Columbia, Canada, South Africa, Kenya, India, and Myanmar. They were often established to serve settlers, workers, and soldiers, helping to spread European pub culture throughout the world.

Nowadays, in Europe alone, the English pub model, with its dark wooden counter, can be found everywhere. Thousands of establishments exist in Europe, each with local, regional, or national variations.

These friendly places have gained in popularity in big cities, where a broad selection of foreign beers is widely consumed. But pub tradition isn't limited to drinking; it also includes entertainment, such as billiards, darts competitions, rock and Celtic music, live performances, piano battles, friendly chats, and more. You can also enjoy the relaxed and welcoming atmosphere while watching football or rugby matches on big screens.

Despite today's challenges, some pubs have bounced back by installing a brewery on site, becoming brewpubs, producing beers for themselves and others or becoming players on the "new scene." Modernized pubs attract a diverse public, perpetuating the tradition of drinking together. These beers, brewed on site using traditional or revamped techniques, are a real asset. They set these establishments apart from traditional pubs, linked to large groups that supply standardized, boring beers.

Many craft microbreweries have seized the opportunity. Their momentum with draft beer, even if limited, could pave the way for a revival of pubs in the 21st century.

Cocktail bars

Since their creation, bars have been special places for socializing and chatting, where people share the latest news and discuss everything under the sun. In France, bistrots, bars, and cafés symbolize French culture and lifestyle. Sipping a coffee or enjoying a good beer, or even a beer cocktail on a terrace, celebrates the good life, friendship, and simplicity, and embodies freedom, lightheartedness, and joie de vivre.

Today's cocktail bars play a central role in the development and advancement of cocktail culture.

Here are a few aspects that prove that these establishments are crucial to the development of this new era of creative drinks:

- **Innovation and creativity:** these are innovation laboratories where bartenders are constantly exploring new combinations of ingredients, preparation techniques, and presentations, pushing traditional boundaries by experimenting with unexpected flavors and aromas, artisanal infusions, and creative garnishes.
- **Customer experience:** these locations focus on the total customer experience. From the atmosphere to the aesthetics of the drinks, every element is carefully designed to create a memorable moment. Customizing cocktails according to the consumer's choices has become the norm, strengthening the bond between bartender and customer.
- **Revival of the classics:** while exploring new avenues, contemporary cocktail bars place great emphasis on revisiting the classics. They revive old recipes with a modern twist, enhancing the heritage of mixology while reinterpreting it for contemporary palates.
- **Training and education:** many of them share their knowledge and passion with the public and professionals alike, organizing training courses, workshops, tastings, and special events to educate customers about the history of spirits, mixology techniques, and the art of tasting.
- **Highlighting quality ingredients:** these bars emphasize the use of quality ingredients, premium spirits, fresh local produce and artisanal syrups, not only improving the quality of the drinks, but also supporting a more sustainable approach to mixology.
- **Collaboration and networking:** the cocktail bar community is interconnected, fostering collaboration between establishments and inter-professional mixology exchanges, creating a dynamic network where ideas circulate, promoting innovation everywhere.
- **Adapting to trends**: cocktail bars are responsive to changing trends in culinary culture and consumer preferences. Whether it's alternative preparation methods, exotic ingredients, or innovative technologies, they remain at the forefront.

In short, today's cocktail bars are the pioneers of this new era of creativity and excellence in the world of drinks.

They shape our perception, appreciation, and experience of cocktails, elevating the art to new heights.

THE HISTORY OF THE COCKTAIL

The exact origin of the word “cocktail,” fraught with false leads and embellished with illusory “maybes,” remains uncertain and subject to several theories.

Nevertheless, there are some certainties about its provenance and original use, which can definitively establish a starting point, even if it dates back to a distant period. There are many legends, hypotheses, and folkloric anecdotes about the origin of the word “cocktail,” some of which seem plausible, but none of which can be proven with certainty.

The legend: the rooster’s tail

HERE ARE THE STORIES RELATED TO THE ROOSTER’S TAIL: COCK-TAIL
A legend links the word “cocktail” to the terms “cock” and “tail,” meaning “rooster’s tail,” linked to the custom of putting a rooster’s feather in the glass, particularly in the USA during Prohibition, to indicate glasses containing alcohol.

Another version tells of a cabaret owner’s daughter who lost her pet rooster and decided to reward the one who found it with a drink she named “cocktail.” The multicolored feathers of a rooster’s tail are also reminiscent of the various colors and shades that make up a cocktail.

The legend: the dregs

HERE’S THE STORY BEHIND THE DREGS SERVED ON TAP: COCK-TAILING
In colonial times, spirits were stored in barrels in taverns. When the barrels were almost empty, bar owners would mix the leftover rum and brandy, known as “tailings,” and sell them at a reduced price.

This cheaper, lower-quality alcohol was sold to customers who knew the going rate and wanted a drink “on tap” from the remains of the barrels.

The liqueur served in this way was known as “the cock.” Thus, customers who wanted a cheap drink could simply order a “cock-tailing.”

First appearance

The very first written appearance of the word "cocktail" can be found in the English satirical newspaper *The Morning Post & Gazetteer,* dated 1798. This anti-government article contains a list of drinks consumed by certain lawmen, including William "the Younger" Pitt, then British Prime Minister. But this slang word does not seem to have the current meaning of a drink made with spirits mixed with other ingredients, as it is noted next to the word: "vulgary called ginger."

It's possible that the word cocktail mentioned here is simply a non-alcoholic drink flavored with ginger, due to its low price, and named "cocktail" because the term ginger seemed to be used at the time to refer to red-feathered roosters.

What do spices and horses have to do with it?

Let's take a closer look at the link to ginger . . .

In the 18th century, the word "cocktail" was also used in another context, referring to a horse that was not a thoroughbred.

John Badcock, an English sportswriter specializing in boxing and horse racing, made several references to this "equine cocktail" in his writings of the 1820s. He also wrote in *Sportman's Slang* in 1825, probably referring to the drink: "The cocktail is ginger." The word is used by other writers, as well as in American equestrian circles in the 1800s.

The first clue is a text from the *London Morning Chronicle* of 1776 about two apothecaries from Baston in Lincolnshire, England, who explained: "As a ginger will make an old horse cock his tail, that an hor's tail cock'd cuts a noble appearance."

The expression "cock his tail" is used to describe a horse's tail, like a rooster's tail.

It's possible that, given that horses had their tails raised like roosters, some drinkers had the idea of calling their ginger-based beverage a "cocktail," because of the stimulating and exciting effects it had on them.

Another mention of the word "cocktail" appears in a poem from 1789's *The Prelateiad, or, the Rape of the Holy Bottle,* alluding to the aphrodisiac virtues of "cocktail," but this time referring to another spice: cayenne pepper.

The shameful link with horses

In the 18th century, English aristocrats used to cut or notch their horses' tails to distinguish them from those of commoners. After the abolition of privileges, this practice became widespread in the hope of appearing richer. Horses other than thoroughbreds took on a livelier, more dashing air.

Another equally distasteful use was made during this period. In his 1785 *A Classical Dictionary of the Vulgar Tongue*, English lexicographer Francis Grose describes the verb "to feague" as follows:

Firm up a horse's muscles to make it bold and make it lift its tail by inserting a piece of ginger or pepper into its rear as a suppository.

Another name variant is "cock-tailed horses." The name "cocktail-horses," meaning "cock-tailed horses," was then coined.

Eighteenth-century horse dealers used to do this before showing their poor beasts for sale, as a raised tail was the sign of a spirited horse that would fetch a higher price. Grose explains that the term is used figuratively to "stimulate, invigorate and energize." Ginger and pepper were also used to improve the taste of certain alcoholic beverages and stimulate the palate. This explains why the term "cocktail" was associated with this type of mix.

The certainty that "feaging" and "cocktail" are related is provided by a satirical article in an English provincial newspaper dating from 1790, where the author uses the terms "cock" and "tail" figuratively, stating: "Hath been guilty of monopolizing all the ginger and the pepper in the neighborhood to make the asses who vote for Sir Gerald Vanneck cock their tails."

It's clear that there is a link between the terms "feaging" and "cocktail," both literally and figuratively. In any case, it's hardly surprising that those who practiced feaging were discreet about it, because if it were discovered, it would have lost its usefulness and largely tainted the equestrian sports world.

When you think about it, it's obvious – ginger is a spice that was used to "invigorate" old horses. The cocktail thus became a "tonic drink," enhanced by the addition of ginger.

This gives you the origin of the word "cocktail" and its link to horses and ginger.

This makes it easy to understand why a Buck (inspired by "bucking horse") is a category of spirit-based drinks mixed with ginger and soda, and why adding ginger ale to cognac results in a Horse's Neck. And the same logic applies when ginger beer is added to vodka to make a Moscow Mule.

NEW HORSE'S NECK

EQUIPMENT

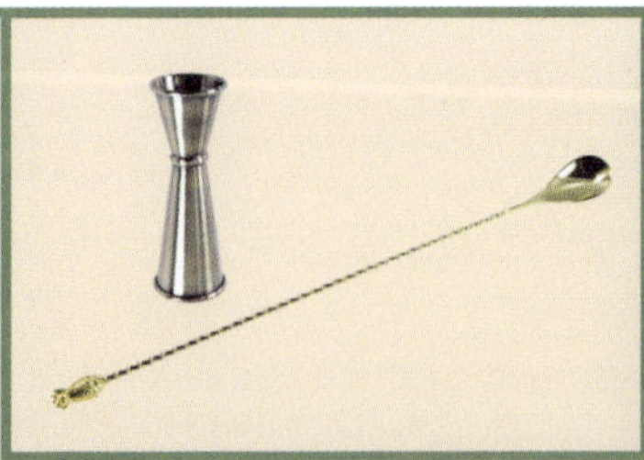

GLASS TYPE: LONG DRINK

DID YOU KNOW? Dating back to the late 19th century, Horse's Neck was originally a non-alcoholic ginger ale, later fortified with bourbon, rye or brandy. It takes its name from the long lemon peel rolled up inside the glass.

INGREDIENTS:

- 1⅓ fl oz (40 ml) cognac Premier Cru (Maison Ferrand)
- ⅓ fl oz (10 ml) cane sugar syrup (Monin)
- BEER: Gose or a sour classic
- Ice
- 1 long orange peel

BUILD IN THE GLASS

1 – Place the ice and all ingredients in the glass, except for the beer, and stir.

2 – Top with beer, stir.

MOSCOW MULE

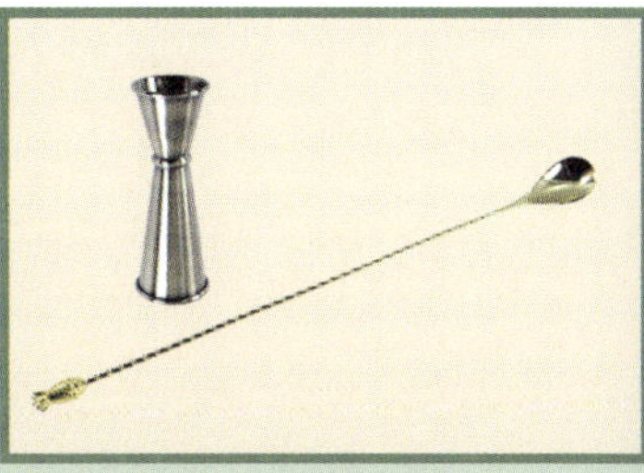

EQUIPMENT

GLASS TYPE: COPPER MUG

DID YOU KNOW? The mule family, served in a copper mug, traditionally uses ginger beer. The best known, the Moscow Mule, combines vodka and spicy ginger beer, the name "Moscow" referring to Russia, and "mule" to the pungent, hoof-like sensation of ginger.

INGREDIENTS:

- 1⅓ fl oz (40 ml) Mermaid Dry gin
- ⅔ fl oz (20 ml) lemon juice
- 2 fl oz (60 ml) ginger tonic or ginger beer (not ginger ale)
- BEER: SpontanBasil (Lindemans Brewery)
- 1 lime
- Grated ginger
- Mint leaves
- Crushed ice

BUILD IN THE GLASS

1 – Fill the glass with crushed ice.

2 – Add the gin and lemon juice and top with tonic, then beer, stir.

3 – Garnish: lime wedge, grated ginger and mint leaves.

In England, the term "cocktail" used to refer to ginger, or sometimes cayenne pepper, used as stimulants in drinks. In 1828, John Badcock in the *Fancy Gazette* mentioned that sports enthusiasts added "a peel or two of cock-tail" to beer (which may be where ginger beer comes from), gin or a mixture of the two.

Here, the designation of ginger is in line with the *Morning Post & Gazetteer* quote from 1798: a ginger-based beverage used as a spice.

In America, however, the term "cocktail," referring to spices as well as pepper and ginger, spread through apothecaries to include all spicy drinks.

Second appearance

The second reference to the word "cocktail" as a beverage appears in an 1803 article published in the American newspaper *The Farmer's Cabinet*. It describes a man soothing his hangover with a cocktail, illustrating the old practice of "curing evil with evil," advocating drinking alcohol in the morning to reduce symptoms!

Around 1806, ginger and cayenne pepper were replaced by bitters, which are more pleasant and kept better. Thus, the very British Gin & Bitter evolved into the typically American "gin cocktail," often drunk as a morning beverage during the first 50 years of its history.

ANTOINE AMÉDÉE PEYCHAUD

This freemason, pharmacist, and apothecary from Bordeaux, who had settled in Saint-Domingue, fled the slave revolt of 1795 and took refuge in New Orleans. Initially for medicinal purposes, he created Peychaud bitter, an aromatic bitter made from gentian and citrus peel, based on a family recipe. To sweeten the bitter beverage, he mixed it with sugar, water, and cognac, and served it in an egg cup, used to measure alcohol. This "medicine" was so successful that his patients often asked him for an "egg cup." This may explain how the word became "cocktail" in taverns near his pharmacy.

Bitters in cocktails

Many drinks, like Campari, can be enjoyed neat or mixed with soda, ice water, gin, or vermouth. From its very beginnings, the cocktail was closely linked to bitters. Although herbal tinctures and remedies have been around for centuries, mixing them with alcohol didn't begin until the 18th century.

From that time on, bitters was a key ingredient, quickly followed by a multitude of elixirs and advertisements in London newspapers. The earliest trace of bitters, dating from 1690, is Elixir Magnum Stomachicum by apothecary Richard Stoughton, sold in his South London dispensary.

Stoughton's Bitters, made from around 20 plants, roots, herbs, and barks, were originally additives for sweet wine or beer. In his advertisements, Richard Stoughton urged people to consume them with wine or brandy as a hangover cure, which brings us closer to the 1803 definition, and makes him its potential inventor. In the 17th century, Purl Royal became a popular drink. The forerunner of modern vermouth, it was made with a base of sweet sherry fortified with brandy and infused with botanicals.

The legend: the egg cup, a story of misunderstanding

According to the most common account, the word "cock-tail" comes from the word "coquetier," used by a French bartender to serve a bitter-based drink in an egg cup. The English, not understanding French, mispronounced "coquetier" as "coquetiel" or "cocktay," to become "cocktail."

Thus, the name of the mixed drink comes from a linguistic error, referring to the particular container used to serve it. This story is reminiscent of that of Antoine Amédée Peychaud. It's possible that the bartender in question, working near Antoine's apothecary, adopted his popular recipe and the way he served it, in an egg cup, to boost his sales.

UNUSUAL PURL

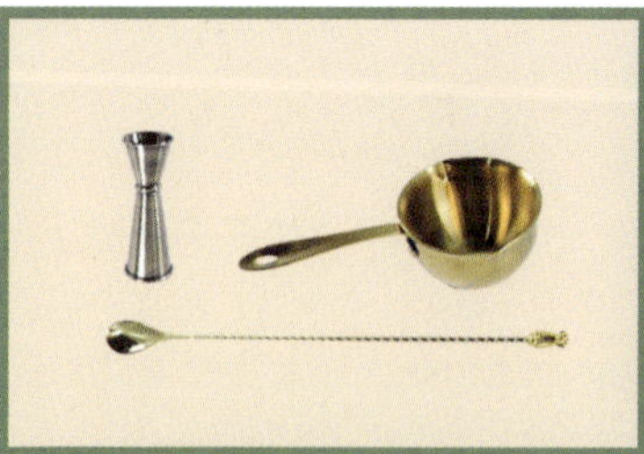

EQUIPMENT

GLASS TYPE: TODDY MUG OR CUP

DID YOU KNOW? Enjoyed as early as the 17th century, especially by workers for its stomach-soothing properties, Purl was often consumed early in the morning. Sold by Purl-men on the Thames in England, it was originally a bitter beer infused with sea wormwood, replaced around a hundred years later by gin and enriched with various spices, including ginger, and sugar.

INGREDIENTS:

- 1⅓ fl oz (40 ml) Old Tom gin or compound gin
- ⅔ fl oz (20 ml) maple syrup
- A dash of Angostura orange bitters
- BEER: use a beer with hints of cider or an apple-flavored Wils sour
- Orange peel
- Caramel shard

BUILD IN THE GLASS

1 – Heat the beer in a saucepan without boiling.
2 – Add the maple syrup, stirring until it dissolves.
3 – Serve the mixture hot, add the gin and bitters and stir.
4 – Garnish: orange peel and a caramel shard.

SAZEREC SPIRIT

GLASS TYPE: COUPE GLASS

DID YOU KNOW? Sazerac, invented in the mid-1800s at the Sazerac Coffee House in New Orleans, originally used Sazerac de Forge & Fils cognac. Due to the shortage of brandy caused by the phylloxera epidemic that ravaged French vineyards at the end of the 19th century, the recipe was modified to include rye whisky. Between the mid-18th and 19th centuries, although their use varied, gin, brandy and wine mixed with bitters gained in popularity on both sides of the Atlantic.

INGREDIENTS:

- 1⅔ fl oz (50 ml) Hennessy cognac
- 1 tsp (5 ml) white absinthe
- 1 dash of Peychaud bitters
- ⅓ fl oz (10 ml) of wheat beer (if possible, aged in a sweet wine barrel) or a barleywine syrup
- Ice
- Lemon peel

IN A MIXING GLASS

1 – Make a cold syrup with the beer (3⅓ fl oz [100 ml] of beer per ¼ cup [50 g] of sugar).

2 – Fill the coupe glass with ice to cool, add absinthe for flavor and set aside.

3 – Pour the other ingredients into the mixing glass and stir.

4 – Empty the absinthe and ice from the cup and pour in the cocktail.

5 – Garnish: a little lemon peel.

Between the mid-18th and 19th centuries, although their use varied, gin, brandy, and wine mixed with bitters gained popularity on both sides of the Atlantic.

First definition of the word cocktail

The very first official definition of the word "cocktail" appeared in 1806 in *The Balance Columbian & Repository*, explaining that the cocktail, often called a Bittered Sling, is a stimulating liquor, composed of a spirit of any kind, water, bitters, and sugar. Nowadays, it's called an Old Fashioned, due to the rise of vermouths and the appearance of neo-cocktails at the end of the 19th century.

As early as the 1820s, numerous references to the cocktail emerged in literature and the press. Despite its reputation as a vulgar drink, it gained in popularity, gradually moving away from its original bitter recipe.

Punch: the first cocktail

The history of cocktails is complex, peppered with anecdotes and varied interpretations. Exploring how recipes have traveled and evolved over time, forming the diversity of cocktails we enjoy today, is fascinating. Long before the word "cocktail" was invented, punch, a mixture of alcohol and other ingredients, captivated British colonists in Southeast Asia as early as the 17th century.

The original punch, named after the Hindi word "paanch," meaning "five," was made with five ingredients: arrack (a local alcohol made from fruit, rice, sugar cane, or palm sap), sugar, water, citrus juice, and spices.

The English, who were very active in Indian trade at the time, imported the recipe to England, where it quickly became a great success. And so punch spread far beyond India's borders.

The British colonies in the Caribbean adopted and adapted the traditional punch, adding the iconic local ingredient: rum. This evolution shows how drinks and recipes have traveled and evolved around the world, forming the diversity of today's cocktails.

BILLY DAWSON PUNCH

EQUIPMENT

SIGNATURE COCKTAIL – BAPTISTE VASSY

GLASS TYPE: BOWL

DID YOU KNOW? John Sinclair claimed in 1807 that "half a pint of strong old ale poured into a moderate bowl of punch would considerably soften the fire of liquor." Many skilled punch makers of the time considered this practice a tour de force. Billy Dawson, "the only man who could brew punch," was one of them.

INGREDIENTS:

- 10 fl oz (300 ml) rum Original Dark Plantation
- 5 fl oz (150 ml) cognac Pure Organic VSOP (A. de Fussigny)
- 10 fl oz (300 ml) boiling water
- A few peeled lemon wedges (or 6 fl oz [180 ml] juice); reserve the peel for garnish (optional)
- BEER: Double Stout (Shepherd Neame brewery)
- 4 oz (120 g) brown sugar
- Nutmeg

BUILD IN THE GLASS

1 – In a bowl, mash the peeled lemon wedges with the sugar, then remove the wedges.
2 – Pour in the boiling water, stirring with a whisk until the sugar has dissolved.
3 – Add the spirits, ending with the beer, and stir.
4 – Garnish: lemon peel and a little grated nutmeg.

From apothecary to mixologist

Colonial expansions resulted in the discovery of new ingredients, which stimulated advancements in herbal medicine. Distillation produced strong alcohols used as preservatives and antiseptics said to improve mental well-being. Alchemists refined the art of distillation, creating herbal or fruity elixirs, such as brandy, Chartreuse, Bénédictine, aquavit, and gin.

The evolution of the cocktail

In the 1850s, cocktails were standardized and served cold, incorporating syrups and other ingredients, as sugar cubes did not dissolve well in cold alcohol, resulting in a subtle but constant change in the cocktail. When Jerry Thomas began writing his *Bartenders Guide* in 1862, he mentioned numerous cocktails, and the list continued to grow. Many books on cocktails were published, stimulating the creativity of bartenders, whose techniques and presentations developed over time.

In the United States, Prohibition (1920–1933) was a major catalyst in the evolution of the cocktail, as the illegality of alcohol led to speakeasies and clandestine drinking. This period gave rise to many unusual and original cocktails. In those days, to hide the mediocrity of contraband alcohol, bartenders used tricks like dilution, the use of creams, strong syrups and fruit to mask flaws and avoid police detection, also resorting to strong, pleasant ingredients like absinthe and chartreuse to improve the taste.

This period encouraged the use of premium ingredients in cocktails, such as juices and fresh fruit. After Prohibition, with the legal resumption of alcohol sales, the fine cocktail industry enjoyed a renaissance, and cocktail culture flourished.

SIDECAR IN HOLLYWOOD

EQUIPMENT

GLASS TYPE: SOUR GLASS

DID YOU KNOW? Paris or London, the origin of the Sidecar remains unclear. Symbolizing the elegance of the Roaring Twenties, this Prohibition cocktail marked the rise of cocktail culture in France.

INGREDIENTS:

- 1⅓ fl oz (40 ml) 12-Year-Old Borderies Cognac (Park)
- ⅔ fl oz (20 ml) triple sec (Cointreau)
- 1 tsp (5 ml) orange syrup (Monin)
- BEER: Gose to Hollywood (To Øl Brewery)
- Orange peel
- Ice

IN THE SHAKER

1 – Add all ingredients except beer and garnish.
2 – Fill with ice and shake.
3 – Serve through a double strainer.
4 – Top with beer, stir.
5 – Garnish: large orange peel.

Between 1950 and 1960, Tiki bars, with their tropical cocktails served in stylized containers, became very popular in the USA. These cocktails, often based on rum, coconut cream, and pineapple or mango juice, embodied exoticism and escapism.

APOCALYPSE PARADISE

EQUIPMENT

GLASS TYPE: TIKI

DID YOU KNOW? The alcohol creates a complex, powerful base with botanical, herbaceous, spice, caramel, vanilla and oak notes. Pineapple juice and coconut cream add tropical sweetness. Lemon juice balances, amarena cherry syrup adds sugar and fruit, and the beer adds tart, caramelized and woody tones.

INGREDIENTS:

- 1⅓ fl oz (40 ml) Raspberry white rum (Botafogo)
- 1⅓ fl oz (40 ml) Elixier gin
- A few pieces of pineapple (or 1⅓ fl oz [40 ml] juice)
- ⅔ fl oz (20 ml) lemon juice
- ⅓ fl oz (10 ml) Amarena cherry syrup
- BEER: Imperial Berliner Weisse with roasted pineapple aged in rum barrels (Apocalypse Brewery)
- 1 tbsp coconut cream
- 1 slice of candied pomelo
- 1 Amarena cherry
- Edible pansies
- Ice

IN THE SHAKER

1 – In a shaker, crush the pineapple chunks.
2 – Add the remaining ingredients, except the beer and garnishes, and do an initial dry shake.
3 – Fill the shaker with ice and shake it again.
4 – Serve by double filtering, top up with beer, stir.
5 – Garnish: a slice of candied pomelo, an Amarena cherry, edible flowers.

CIGARITA

EQUIPMENT

GLASS TYPE: COUPE GLASS

DID YOU KNOW? Margaret Sames, an American socialite, is said to have created the margarita in Acapulco in 1948 to liven up a party. The name "Margarita" was chosen in her honor.

INGREDIENTS:

- 1⅓ fl oz (40 ml) Blanco Volcan tequila
- ⅔ fl oz (20 ml) triple sec (Maison Ferrand)
- ⅔ fl oz (20 ml) lemon juice
- 1 fl oz (30 ml) whole milk
- BEER: Gose Margarita (Cigar City Brewery)
- 1 slice of lime
- Pink salt

PREPARE IN A MIXING GLASS

1 – Rim the coupe glass by dipping it in lemon juice, then in pink salt.
2 – Make a clarified milk punch: pour all the ingredients except the milk and lime slice into the mixing glass and stir.
3 – Pour whole milk into a container and add the first mixture to the milk (not the other way round).
4 – Wait at least 45 minutes for the mixture to curdle.
5 – Pour into a coffee filter over the mixing glass and wait until it has all been filtered. Filter several times if needed.
6 – Serve.
7 – Garnish: a slice of lime.

At the beginning of the 21st century, cocktail culture evolved significantly with the impetus of "innovative cocktails," blending fresh ingredients, innovative techniques and classics, giving rise to exclusive and refined cocktails. This has revived interest in classic cocktails and the consumption of high-end spirits from small producers, as well as rare liqueurs and artisanal bitters.

For years, the craze for refined cocktails has popularized mixology, enriching and modernizing the experience. Derived from "mix" and "logos" (science), mixology is today a discipline in its own right that redefines cocktails, making them more contemporary and high-quality.

This trend towards creative cocktails marked the advent of the "mixology movement," with the application of expertise and the use of unusual ingredients, such as balsamic vinegars, smoked chilies, and local organic produce.

It promotes local produce and adopts an eco-responsible approach, emphasizing the use of all ingredients to minimize waste. For example, leftover citrus pulp can be turned into syrups and peel into garnishes, reducing waste.

More and more health-conscious people are turning to alternatives to alcoholic beverages, sparking a growing interest in "mocktails." These healthier, non-alcoholic drinks combine fruit, vegetables, flavored waters, granita, edible flowers, herbs, and spices. Every detail is carefully thought out to dazzle the senses.

Cocktails are becoming more modern, using chemistry, textures, and captivating colors. They become seductive works of art with authentic flavors.

Modern mixology, a blend of art, science and creativity, constantly pushes the boundaries, offering memorable tasting experiences. It's an ideal time for cocktail lovers and connoisseurs to explore mixology innovations. At the same time, "flair," the elegant art of acrobatically manipulating ingredients and equipment, is evolving into a distinct discipline.

An essential part of modern culture, contemporary mixology often contrasts with traditional bartending. At the same time, traditional and vintage cocktails are making a comeback, with bartenders striving to meticulously recreate the flavors of a bygone era.

Advances in products and equipment

Talking about the evolution of cocktails also means talking about the advances in products and equipment. An excellent bartender must use quality products and remain open to innovation to avoid boredom and maintain creativity.

Brands support this progress by offering innovative, high-quality products that encourage further exploration. Innovation is crucial, even for the best, and progress without the support of brands introducing new products is difficult. It's important to note that not everyone has the skills or resources to create homemade products.

Can you excel behind a bar with just a jigger and a shaker? Yes – but mixology tools, inspired in particular by cooking, have evolved to such an extent that it would be a shame not to use them. New methods such as vacuum distillation, cold infusion, clarification, and molecular mixology with advanced equipment such as flavorers, blenders, smoking cloches, and pipettes have emerged. Some modern bars even use ready-made cocktails, eliminating the need for shakers.

PURITY

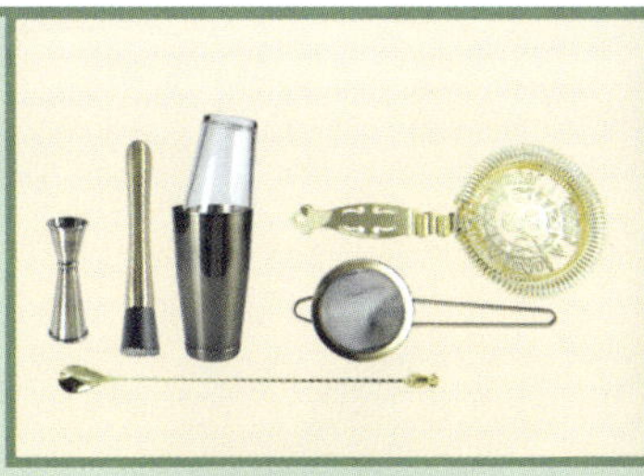

EQUIPMENT

GLASS TYPE: TASTING

INGREDIENTS:

- 1⅓ fl oz (40 ml) White Cane Spirit (Lyre's)
- A few pieces of white peach (or 1 fl oz [30 ml] juice)
- ⅓ fl oz (10 ml) rose syrup (Monin)
- ⅓ fl oz (10 ml) squeezed lemon juice
- BEER: Implosion (To Øl Brasserie)
- 1 snapdragon

IN THE SHAKER

1 – Mash the white peach pieces in a shaker.
2 – Add all ingredients except beer and snapdragon, fill with ice and shake.
3 – Serve through a double strainer.
4 – Top with beer, stir.
5 – Garnish: snapdragon.

MIXOLOGY BASICS

Mixology requires specific tools for the precise creation of cocktails. It's crucial to choose from a variety of shakers, spoons, dosers, and strainers, taking into account your aesthetic preferences, budget, and ease of use. There are five main approaches to mixing a cocktail – "build in the glass," the shaker, the blender, throwing, and the mixing glass. It is possible to mix a cocktail without a shaker or measure without a jigger. Here are the essential accessories for getting started in mixology.

Build in the glass

To prepare a drink "in the glass" means mixing the ingredients directly into it. This simple method avoids the use of unnecessary utensils. For a fizzy cocktail, add the ingredients, fill with ice, stir to dilute and refresh, then top with soda at the end to preserve the fizz. To retain the bubbles, gently stir the ice cubes at the bottom with a mixing spoon.

Shaker

The shaker is an iconic tool used to vigorously shake cocktail ingredients, chilling, aerating, and mixing ingredients of different densities to alter the texture.

How to use it? Hold the shaker firmly in both hands and shake ingredients vigorously, with or without ice, to mix, dilute, and cool effectively. Dilution is essential to the final result, as is the accuracy of the measurements. The length of time you shake varies depending on the type of cocktail.

There are three main types of shakers:

COBBLER SHAKER

Often used at home for its simplicity, it consists of three parts: a large tumbler, a lid with integrated strainer, and sometimes a graduated stopper acting as a measuring cup. Ideal if you don't have a strainer, it allows you to pour the cocktail directly into the glass, filtering out ice cubes and large residues. Be wary of cheap models that get stuck after cooling; shake them horizontally to avoid this.

Opt for stainless steel models, that keep drinks cool, unlike plastic ones, and avoid glass models, which are easily breakable. Despite less fine filtration with the built-in strainer, this tool remains practical and versatile for basic use and is appreciated by novices for its ease of use.

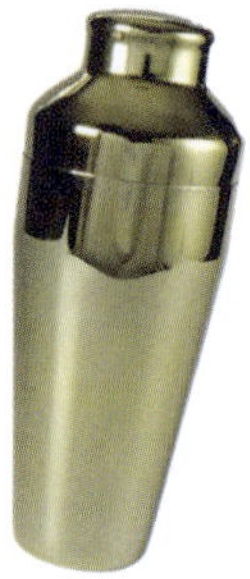

CONTINENTAL OR PARISIAN SHAKER

This sleek, easy-to-handle, streamlined model combines two stainless steel elements: a large cup and a lid, known as the "tin." It provides an airtight seal for consistent mixing and optimal cooling of the cocktail during shaking.

BOSTON SHAKER

Prized for its ease of use and efficiency, this highly fashionable shaker, widely used in bars, includes a large stainless steel cup and a Boston-style mixing glass, available in glass, stainless steel, or plastic.

Blender mixer

Ideal for quickly and evenly mixing the liquid and solid ingredients of certain cocktails such as Piña Coladas or frozen drinks, effectively blending thick ingredients such as fruit, ice cream, and purées for a smooth texture.

Milk foamer

Often used to make milk foam in cafés, it is also invaluable for cocktails to quickly emulsify liquid ingredients, creating a light foam ideal for drinks with egg whites, cream, or milk. It gives a creamy and airy texture, enhancing the mouthfeel and aesthetics with its delicate foam.

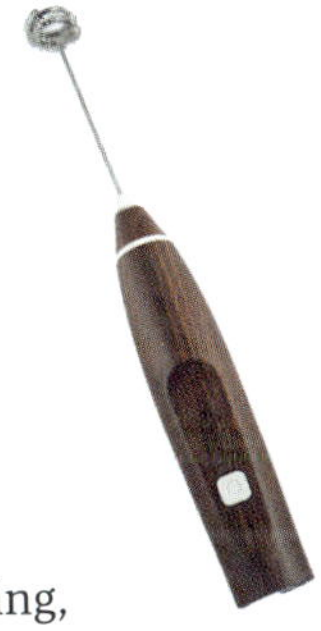

Mixing glass

This is an essential tool for cocktails that require delicate mixing without shaking, preserving the clarity of the drink. If you don't have this tool, a shaker cup or Boston shaker glass can be used. Often thick, in a variety of shapes and sizes, some models are graduated, with or without a spout.

To preserve the delicacy of spirit-based cocktails, use a glass, a mixing spoon and ice to cool without excessive shaking. This method produces a smooth, dense texture, preserving the structure of the ingredients and avoiding excessive dilution. Sleek and elegant, it adds a touch of sophistication to the preparation and presentation of cocktails.

Mixing spoon

Often made of stainless steel, elegant and functional, its long, twisted stem provides a good grip for efficient mixing of ingredients. Its trident, disc, or pestle-shaped end is used to catch or crush ingredients, making it an essential accessory for the careful preparation of cocktails.

Measuring jigger

Accurate measuring of ingredients is crucial to the delicate alchemy of flavors, smells, and textures in each cocktail. An imbalance can spoil the taste experience. The jigger, an essential measuring tool, ensures precise proportions, guaranteeing perfectly balanced cocktails every time.

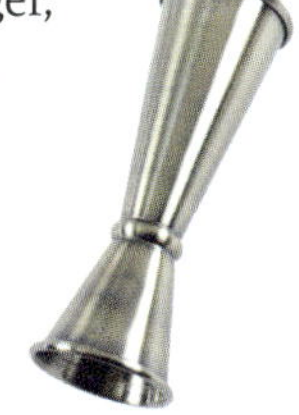

Hawthorne strainer

Very popular for shakers and mixing glasses, it has two or more legs, a perforated plate, and one or two flexible spring strainer springs, which hold back the pieces for a smooth drink.

Julep strainer

Used for stirred cocktails such as the mint julep, it provides precise filtration with its perforated hollow shape. Available in a variety of shapes and sizes, it fits over the mixing glass for direct pouring into the cocktail glass.

In around 1800, it was a large, slotted spoon used to protect teeth from ice in iced drinks, before plastic straws were invented.

Fine strainer or cheesecloth

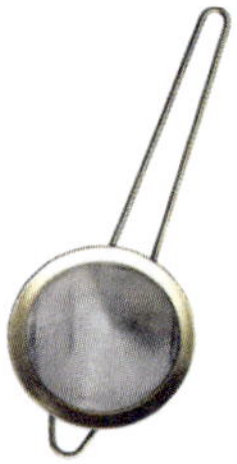

A tight-mesh bar utensil, it finely filters out unwanted bits for a smooth cocktail. Often used in double filtration with another strainer, it is ideal for drinks served "up" requiring a refined texture, poured directly without ice for a fresh taste.

Citrus juicer

Bars often use automatic, electric, or lever-operated citrus juicers for quick and easy squeezing. However, a simple hinged Mexican citrus juicer is all you need to extract the juice from fresh citrus fruit. Always opt for natural juices.

Egg separator

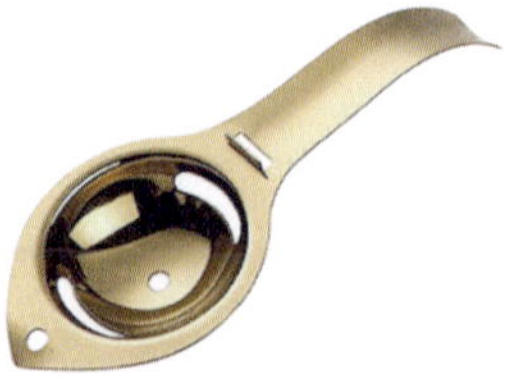

Some cocktails contain egg. Although the shell is often used to separate the white from the yolk, some people prefer other methods to avoid pieces of shell. Note that egg separators and shells are the quickest and most hygienic ways to separate eggs.

Channel knife, zester and grater

Ideal for decorating, the channel knife creates large, coarse ribbons of zest, adding originality and pleasant aromas to cocktails. The blade of the zester, which removes fine citrus peel, creates long ribbons of zest releasing a fragrance of fresh, intense essential oils.

These zests garnish drinks, enhancing both the visual and aromatic experience. The grater makes fine shavings, adding flavor, aroma, and style to your creations. Choose a grater with a receptacle to avoid scattering zest.

Peeler or scraper

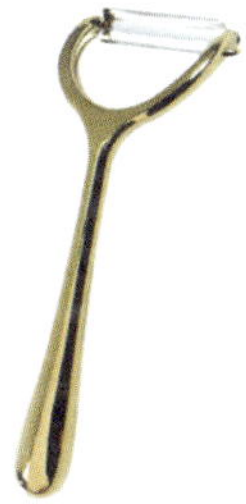

The vegetable peeler is ideal for peeling fruit. Its sharp blade effectively removes the skin with minimal loss of flesh.

Paring knife and cutting board

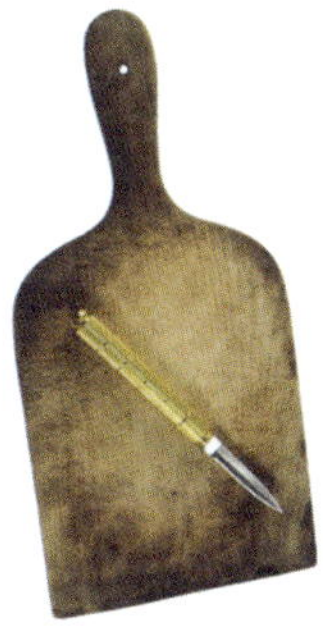

Essential for mixology, the paring knife has a short, sharp blade that is perfect for precise cuts of fruit or zest. Ceramic blades do not corrode with citrus juice but are more fragile.

Useful for working cleanly, glass or stone cutting boards are easy to clean but dull blades. Plastic boards wear out and attract bacteria into the grooves. Wooden boards require regular maintenance but last well. Durable rubber ones are the best option.

Ice spoon, ice twister, and ice bucket

The frequent use of ice cubes in cocktails requires careful handling for hygiene reasons and for efficiency. For greater durability, it is best to use stainless steel ice tongs and an ice scoop. Having an ice bucket nearby improves service by offering accessibility and speed.

Powder shaker

Sprinkling various powders enhances the presentation, adding an elegant visual and taste touch to each creation.

Mortar

Used to crush ingredients, maximizing extraction and aromatic concentration. Use it in the lid of a shaker or a sturdy glass. To avoid the bitterness of fresh herbs and enrich the flavors of the drink, squeeze them by hand rather than crushing them.

Skewers

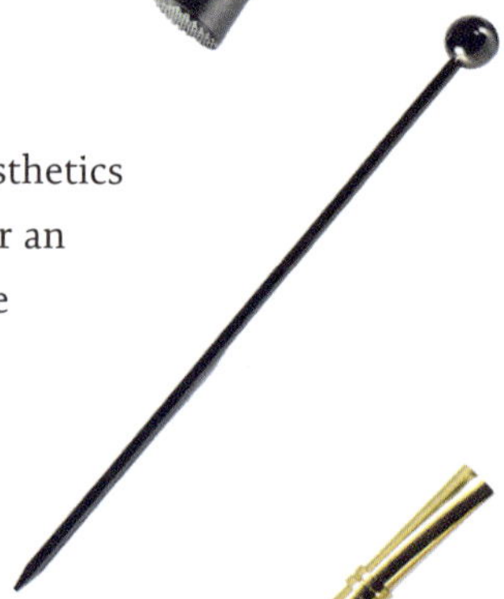

Much more than simple accessories, skewers enhance the aesthetics of cocktails. Used to garnish beverages with style, they offer an attractive and functional presentation, holding decorative ingredients in place. A carefully selected range of skewers reflects the theme of the cocktail and adds an artistic touch.

Straw

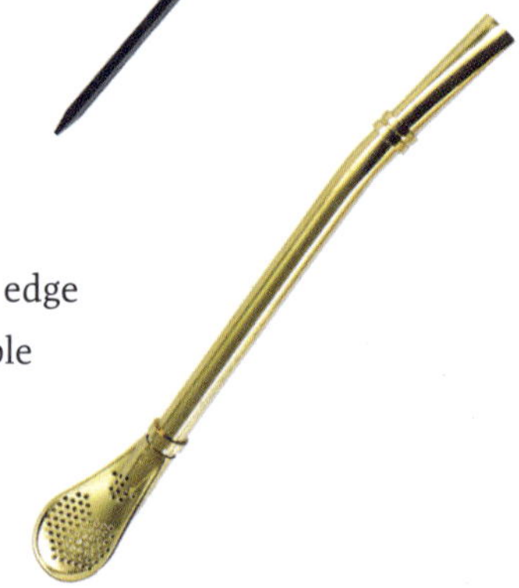

Eco-friendly and durable, metal straws bring a sustainable edge and a touch of elegance to every cocktail, plus they're reusable and easy to clean.

GLASSWARE

The choice of glass is crucial for a cocktail, both to complement the elegance of the drink and to enhance the recipe. With an infinite number of shapes and sizes available, the ideal glass must also maintain the right temperature, ensure comfort when drinking, and promote optimal diffusion of aromas. More than just useful, it adds an aesthetic dimension to the cocktail, enhancing the visual experience. Choosing an elegant glass adds sophistication and highlights the refined character of the drink.

Make sure it's clean and handle it by the stem or base to avoid warming it up and getting it dirty.

There's no need to chill the cocktail and shaker if you're using a warm glass. For a cocktail served without ice, 30 minutes in the freezer will cool it down. Fill it with crushed ice and water for rapid, though less effective, cooling. Conversely, for hot cocktails, warm the glass with hot water, empty it, then pour in the drink.

Glass types

COCKTAIL GLASS

Used for short drinks of 2⅓ fl oz (70 ml) or more, served without ice.

MARTINI:

Capacity: 4–8½ fl oz (120–250 ml)

Conical shape, wide rim, long stem.

Use: perfect for mixed drinks, often served chilled without ice.

MARGARITA:

Capacity: 6–8½ fl oz (180–250 ml)

Rounded shape, wide bowl, shallow with two tiers, often with a flat rim, flared outward, medium stem.

Use: ideal for margaritas and other tequila-based cocktails.

TASTING GLASS

Capacity: 8½ -19½ fl oz (250–580 ml)

Available in various shapes and sizes, it has a generous aromatic chamber and a narrow rim.

Use: perfect for all types of cocktails.

CHAMPAGNE GLASS (COUPE)

Capacity: 4–10 fl oz (120–300 ml)

Wide, shallow shape, medium to long stem.

Use: ideal for high-alcohol short-drink cocktails served without ice.

CHAMPAGNE FLUTE

Capacity: 4½–10 fl oz (140–300 ml)

Tall, narrow, elegant, often slender form, with many shapes and sizes.

Use: often reserved for sparkling drinks, it is also used for sparkling cocktails served without ice.

Each cocktail has its own glass, carefully chosen to enhance its scent, aroma, and presentation, while evoking its history and creating a visual harmony with its delicate shape.

They prolong the cocktail experience, influence the way the drink touches the lips, amplify perceptions, and capture nuances, thus contributing fully to the pleasures of taste. They reveal the bartender's artistic expression, elevating each drink to the status of an ephemeral work of art.

LOWBALL, OLD FASHIONED, WHISKY, ROCKS

Capacity: 6⅔ -11 fl oz (200–330 ml)

Low, wide, sturdy shape, without a stem.

Use: for strong short drinks such as whisky, served on the rocks or mixed.

HIGHBALL

Capacity: 6⅔ –12 fl oz (200–350 ml)
Same shape as the Collins, but a little wider, smaller, and higher than a lowball.
Use: ideal for long-drink cocktails.

COLLINS-TUMBLER

Capacity: 8–13½ fl oz (240–400 ml)
Cylindrical shape, tall and narrow, resembles a tube without a stem.
Use: perfect for refreshing gin-based drinks.

COGNAC

Capacity: 5–23½ fl oz (150–700 ml)
Flared shape with a large aromatic chamber and a narrow rim to better diffuse and retain aromas, short stem.
Use: designed for cognacs and brandies.

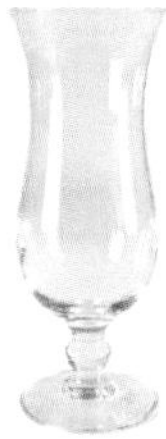

HURRICANE

Capacity: 10–23½ fl oz (300–700 ml)
Thinner and more elongated shape than the tulip glass, with a very short stem.
Use: often used for tropical cocktails and mixed drinks.

TODDY

Capacity: 6–8 fl oz (180–240 ml)
Slightly flared shape with thick walls, often has a handle for easier handling without burning your hands, short stem.
Use: very sturdy, ideal for hot cocktails.

SOUR

Capacity: 5–9 fl oz (150–270 ml)
Flared shape, this small glass often has a small aromatic chamber with a wider rim, medium stem.
Use: can be used for tangy cocktails.

MULE TIMBALE

Capacity: 12–18½ fl oz (350–550 ml)

Hammered copper-plated stainless steel mug shape.

Use: ideal for full-bodied cocktails, served with crushed ice.

JULEP CUP

Capacity: 12–18½ fl oz (350–550 ml)

Conical cup shape with straight stainless steel sides, which helps keep drinks cold.

Use: perfect for cocktails with crushed ice.

BOSTON

Capacity: 9–15 fl oz (270–450 ml)

Conical shape, thick, solid, without a stem, with a wide rim, often used as a tumbler for the Boston shaker, it is designed to withstand shocks.

Use: perfect for mojito-type cocktails.

TIKI

Capacity: 10–20 fl oz (300–600 ml)

Various shapes, often decorated with Tiki motifs.

Use: excellent for tropical drinks.

FANCY

Capacity: 5–20 fl oz (150–600 ml)

Glasses of various shapes and sizes, with a variety of decorations, designed to complement the beauty of the cocktail and add a touch of exoticism to the drink.

SLING

Capacity: 8½–13½ fl oz (250–400 ml)

Conical shape, elongated and thin, widened at the rim, with a small bowl, without a stem.

Use: perfect for long cocktails with crushed ice.

Often overlooked, glasses are essential. They serve not only as containers, but also as functional aesthetic elements, crucial to the tasting experience of each cocktail.

In mixology, glasses are not mere accessories, but essential companions, sculpting the essence of the cocktail and contributing to its beauty. Choosing the right glass creates a visual and taste symphony, elevating the simple act of drinking to a unique sensory experience.

ESSENTIAL INGREDIENTS

Ingredients are the foundation of every cocktail. Each plays its own specific role in creating a harmonious balance.

Spirits form the base, providing the alcoholic structure and defining the cocktail's main character, juices and syrups give sweetness and freshness, while liqueurs and creams add complexity, and sodas ensure effervescence, lightness, and balance.

These essential ingredients each play a key role in the harmony of the cocktail.

Herbs and spices accentuate or contrast the flavors of cocktails, creating a rich and varied taste experience. Beer adds natural effervescence, enriching the texture and providing a unique aromatic depth, making beer-based cocktails popular for their lightness and originality.

Wine-based aperitif

Classified as fortified wines, wine-based aperitifs are enriched with alcohol and sometimes sugar, and may include roots, spices, or bark through maceration, infusion, or flavoring. The main types are vermouth and quinquina.

VERMOUTH

This is not a spirit, but a blend of white or red wine, brandy, sugar, aromatic herbs, and spices that give it its distinctive character. Made with at least 70% white wine aged for one to three years, it must have an alcohol content of between 14.5% and 22% to qualify for the appellation. It can be aged in oak barrels for five to six months.

Before aging, sugar is added to white vermouth or caramel to red vermouth for color. Otherwise, it is classified as "dry," with a generally higher alcohol content, at 18% versus 16%. The main vermouths are categorized according to their sugar content:

- **Dry and Extra Dry:** 18–20%, 1–1¾ oz/34 fl oz (30–50 g/l)
- **Bianco:** 16%, 3½–5 oz/34 fl oz (100–150 g/l)
- **Sweet Rosso:** 15–17%, 5+ oz/34 fl oz (150+g/l)
- **Rosé:** 14.5 to 18%, 3½–5 oz/34 fl oz (100–150 g/l)

DID YOU KNOW?

The use of wormwood leaves is mandatory in its preparation, and its name derives from "wermut," meaning "wormwood" in German.

QUINQUINA

These white or red wine-based aperitifs are enriched with herbs, bitter orange peel, fruit, macerated spices, brandy, sugar, and quinine, a key ingredient named after the bark of the South American cinchona plant. They have a bitter, slightly sweet flavor, valued for their stimulating and digestive properties.

Americano, a type of quinquina, contains wine, alcohol, gentian, sugar, and red or yellow coloring. Gentian, a bitter plant, gives this drink its characteristic flavor.

In cocktails, herbs, sugar, spices, and the bitterness of the wine-based aperitif create a balance without raising the alcohol content too high.

OLD PAL

EQUIPMENT

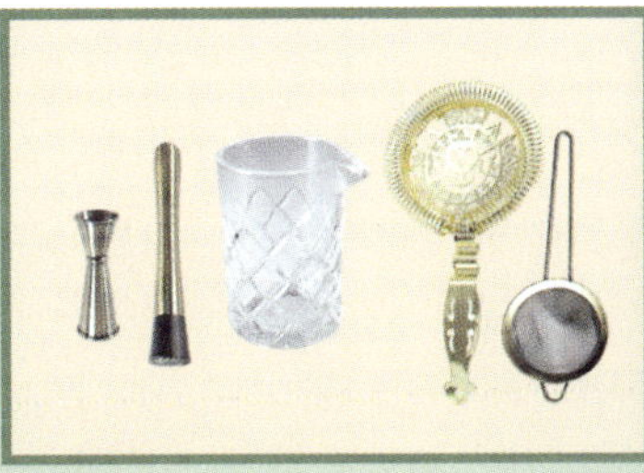

GLASS TYPE: TASTING

INGREDIENTS:

- 1⅓ fl oz (40 ml) Black Wall Rye whisky (Bordeaux Distilling & Co)
- 1 fl oz (30 ml) Noilly Prat
- ⅓ fl oz (10 ml) Sirene Amaro
- A few grapefruit segments (or 1 fl oz [30 ml] juice)
- ⅓ fl oz (10 ml) grapefruit syrup (Monin)
- BEER: Grunion Pale Ale (Ballast Point Brewery)
- Lemon peel
- Ice

IN A MIXING GLASS

1 – Crush a few grapefruit segments in the mixing glass.

2 – Add all ingredients except beer and garnish, fill with ice and stir.

3 – Serve through a double strainer.

4 – Top with beer, stir.

5 – Garnish: lemon peel.

Aperitif bitters (spirits)

There are two main categories of bitters: aperitifs, with an alcohol content of 12% to 40%, enjoyed neat or in cocktails; and cocktail bitters, aromatic concentrates used in small quantities in cocktails.

Originally used as medicinal remedies to aid digestion after meals, bitters and alcoholic aperitifs are characterized by their strong bitterness and often high sugar content. These drinks are enriched with herbs, roots, flowers, spices, or fruit peels infused or macerated in neutral alcohol or other spirits.

Maceration time varies from a few days to several months, depending on composition and desired flavor profile. After infusion, the mixture is often distilled to purify and intensify the flavors. It's common to add caramel for a distinctive color.

Compared to the aromatics of mixology, they are crucial to the creation of modern cocktails. Their wide range of ingredients offers an infinite diversity of flavors and styles, enriching even the most daring cocktails.

These bitters are distinguished by their bitterness, amplifying the flavors of cocktails. They act as flavor enhancers, releasing the aromas of the ingredients for an enriched sensory experience.

TANGY CHILL

EQUIPMENT

GLASS TYPE: OLD FASHIONED

DID YOU KNOW? In the 18th century, apothecaries created herbal bitters for their medicinal properties, treating both indigestion and melancholy. Their stores, centers of knowledge, attracted customers in search of healing and new taste experiences, laying the foundations for modern mixology.

INGREDIENTS:

- 1⅓ fl oz (40 ml) dark rum (Sober Spirit)
- ⅓ fl oz (10 ml) alcohol-free bitters (BTTR)
- ⅓ fl oz (10 ml) squeezed lemon juice
- ⅔ fl oz (20 ml) rum syrup (Monin)
- BEER: non-alcoholic IPA (Jopen Brewery)
- Lime peel
- Ice

IN A MIXING GLASS

1 – Pour all ingredients into the shaker, except the beer.
2 – Fill shaker with ice and shake.
3 – Serve over ice, double filtered.
4 – Top with beer, stir.
5 – Garnish: lime peel.

Cocktail bitters (aromatic essence concentrates)

These are concentrated mixtures of roots, herbs, spices, quinine, and other plants, infused or macerated, used raw, dried, or as extracts, then dissolved in alcohol. They add bitterness, depth, and complexity, with alcohol content ranging from 20% to 44%.

ANGOSTURA

This was created in 1824 by Dr Johann Siegert in Venezuela for medicinal purposes to treat stomach aches and tropical diseases. It quickly became an essential ingredient in cocktails and certain culinary recipes. The production method, kept secret, involves macerating plants and spices such as gentian, orange peel, and cinchona in rum, followed by distillation, resulting in a 44.7% bitter.

PEYCHAUD BITTERS

This Louisiana bitters, created by Creole apothecary Antoine Amédée Peychaud in the late 18th century, is made from 35% neutral alcohol, gentian, herbs, spices, and citrus peel. It reveals notes of anise, mint, a touch of cotton candy, and bubblegum. Essential in the Sazerac cocktail, it remains a cornerstone of mixology.

FLAVORED BITTERS

Many varieties of bitters used in mixology include citrus notes, such as orange, and spices, star anise, and coriander. Others are flavored with cucumber, cherry, or peach, with alcohol contents ranging from 30 to 44%.

Brandy

Brandy is an English term for wine or fermented fruit spirit obtained by distillation. Some liqueurs, although not of wine origin, are called brandy: cherry-brandy, orange-brandy, apricot-brandy, and prune-brandy. Brandy is aged for at least a year in oak barrels, giving it complex woody aromas and an alcohol content of 36–60%.

Brandies can be found all over the world, with regional variations such as Cognac, Armagnac, Calvados, Grappa, or Pisco. The Dutch adopted the highly distinguished cognac in the 15th century, called "brandewijn" or "burnt wine," "brandy" in English and "brandevin" in French, offering notes of dried fruit, vanilla, and wood.

PISCO

This is a South American spirit, produced in Chile and Peru, distilled from fresh grapes fermented without aging in barrels, retaining its clarity and freshness. Its aromatic profile is complex: dry, floral, fruity, slightly spicy notes with a smooth texture.

In Peru, there are two main categories: Pisco Puro, made from a single grape variety; and Pisco Acholado, made from a blend of several grape varieties.

YELLOW PISCO SOUR

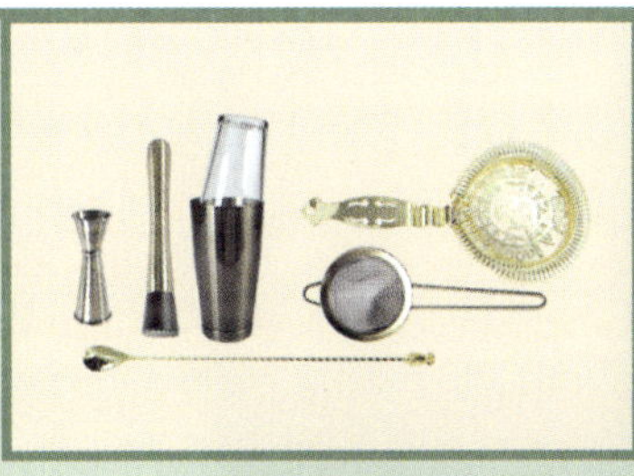

EQUIPMENT

GLASS TYPE: TASTING

INGREDIENTS:

- 1⅓ fl oz (40 ml) El Gobernador Pisco
- ⅔ fl oz (20 ml) Contraluz mezcal
- A few pieces of guava (or 1⅓ fl oz [40 ml] of nectar)
- ⅓ fl oz (10 ml) violet syrup (Monin)
- BEER: Imperial Notorious POG (Stone Brewery)
- 1 egg white
- Pansies
- Ice

IN A MIXING GLASS

1 – Mash a few pieces of guava in a shaker, add all the ingredients except the beer and pansies and give it an initial dry shake.
2 – Fill the shaker with ice and give it another shake.
3 – Serve through a double strainer.
4 – Top with beer, stir.
5 – Garnish: pansies.

ARMAGNAC

Produced in Bas-Armagnac, Haut-Armagnac, and Ténarèze, in south-western France, it is distilled once in a traditional copper still and aged in oak barrels (except for "blanche armagnac") for several years, giving it a rich aromatic complexity of dried fruits, prunes, vanilla, and sometimes flowers and spices. With an alcohol content of between 40 and 45%, this eau-de-vie is popular as an aperitif or digestif. It comes in the following varieties:

- **Blanche armagnac:** little or no aging, retaining its original light color. Often used as a base for cocktails or enjoyed on its own.
- **VS (Very Special):** matured in oak barrels for at least two years, it offers lighter fruity and floral tones than the older versions.
- **VSOP (Very Superior Old Pale):** aged in oak barrels for at least four years, it is highly complex, with notes of dried fruit and spices.
- **XO (Extra Old):** matured in oak barrels for at least ten years, it reveals remarkable richness and depth, with complex aromas of candied fruit, wood, and nuts.

COGNAC

Produced in the Charente region in six appellation zones – Grand Champagne, Petite Champagne, Borderie, Fins Bois, Bons Bois, and Bois Ordinaires – it is distilled from white wine made mainly from Ugni Blanc, Colombard, and Folle Blanche grape varieties.

After distillation, it is aged for at least two years in oak barrels, often longer to develop more complex aromas. Its profile includes notes of dried fruit, vanilla, nuts, and wood, according to the terroir and aging. Appreciated for its finesse and richness, it can be enjoyed neat, on the rocks, or in classic cocktails. Like Armagnac, it is classified as follows:

- **VS (Very Special) or ***:** aged in oak barrels for at least two years, often longer, it offers light fruity and floral tones.
- **VSOP (Very Superior Old Pale) or Reserve**: matured in oak barrels for at least four years, it adds complexity with notes of dried fruit, spices, and vanilla.
- **XO (Extra Old) or Hors d'Âge:** matured in oak barrels for at least ten years. Many XOs age longer, offering remarkable aromatic richness and depth. They are characterized by complex aromas of candied fruit, wood, caramel, and nuts.

- **Napoleon or Extra:** this category falls between VSOP and XO in terms of aging and quality.

CALVADOS

This Norman brandy, distilled from fermented apple or pear cider, has rich, complex aromas. Aged in oak barrels, it reveals woody, vanilla notes. Often drunk as a digestif or used in cocktails, it gives a distinct apple flavor. It is classified according to age and geographical origin:

- **Calvados Pays d'Auge:** AOC (French certification for origin and quality), imposing strict production standards, such as the use of specific apples and traditional distillation methods.

- **Calvados Domfrontais:** the appellation designates a calvados produced specifically in the south-western Orne region of Normandy, where distillation includes a blend of apples and pears (30%).
- **Calvados hors d'âge:** this calvados, matured in oak barrels for at least six years, develops additional complexity and aromatic richness.
- **Calvados VS, VSOP, XO:** these terms designate different types of aging: VS (Very Special) for a minimum of two years, VSOP (Very Superior Old Pale) for four years, and XO (Extra Old) for calvados aged at least six years.

Cordial

An alcohol-free liquid, less sweet than syrups, cordial is used diluted in water or in cocktails. Historically, in the United States, this term referred to liqueurs. Today, it refers to a syrup balanced in acidity, bitterness, and sugar.

Like a syrup, it's made with sugar, water, and often fresh citrus juice, adding acidity and freshness while improving shelf life. Certain essential oils are sometimes added to reinforce the acidity of the fruit and enrich the character of the ingredients, thus binding the flavors of the drinks. Although all cordials are syrups, syrups are not necessarily cordials, differing in their more complex preparation and aroma.

SQUASH

Non-alcoholic English creation made from a concentrate of fruit juice, water, sugar, and sometimes plant extracts, with an average juice content of 30%, although some contain as little as 20%. More fluid than traditional syrup, it easily dilutes in water or beer. Frequently used ingredients are citrus fruits such as oranges, limes, and lemons, or a mix of fruits, flowers, and berries, such as blackcurrants or elderflowers. Modern squashes may also contain additional flavorings and food colorings.

SHRUB

This is a purée of cooked fruit or vegetables, often enriched with spices and oil, then diluted with vinegar to create a sweet-tart syrup, also known as drinking vinegar. Used in mixology to add complexity and acidity to cocktails, it is usually obtained by macerating fruit in vinegar and sugar, before filtering to obtain a ready-to-use shrub. It can be used as a main ingredient or as an aromatic complement to add a tangy, fruity touch to drinks.

OLEO-SACCHARUM

Its name means "sugar oil." This method dates back to the early 19th century and involves extracting essential oils from citrus peels by maceration with sugar. After extraction, the mixture is diluted with water to form a syrup. It is sometimes enriched with vegetable juices or spices, offering more complex flavors than classic syrups. This method was born out of the seasonal scarcity of citrus fruits, allowing bartenders to create an intense concoction that enhances cocktails.

Gin

Originally from the Netherlands, gin is derived from genever, a spirit that originated in 15th-century Dutch Flanders. This grain and malt wine distillate was flavored with juniper berries, used specifically to mask the flaws of primitive distillation. Adopted by the English army in Holland during the Thirty Years' War for its medicinal and battle-stimulating properties, it was nicknamed "Dutch courage." After William III banned imports of foreign spirits in 1688, the English began producing their own gin.

In early 17th-century England, interest in "genever water," also known as "genever" and then "gin," spread beyond soldiers returning from war, especially after the monopoly of the London distillers' guild ended in 1690 with the Distilling Act.

Modern gin, with a minimum alcohol content of 37.5%, distilled from cereals such as rye or barley, or molasses, can be flavored with spices, herbs, and fruit, naturally or artificially. Juniper, an essential ingredient, is added naturally or chemically. There is a wide variety of gins listed below.

GENEVER

The Dutch ancestor of gin, made from malt grains, it offers a sweeter, richer flavor profile than traditional gin, which is mostly juniper flavored. Other herbs and spices can be added. There are two variants: "Jonge" (young), with a lighter taste, and "Oude" (old), which is richer.

COMPOUNDING

Flavored after a single distillation with essences or plant extracts, it is less complex, ideal for cocktails where finesse is not crucial.

DISTILLED GIN

This gin incorporates botanical ingredients directly during distillation, allowing the aromas to infuse fully. This method produces a high-quality gin with superior aromatic complexity.

LONDON GIN

Famous for its dry profile and predominance of juniper, London Dry Gin is renowned for its purity and quality. No artificial flavors or colors are added after distillation, except for a small amount of sugar.

NEW WESTERN GIN

Often associated with American distilleries, it encourages innovation with bold vegetal notes, sometimes minimizing juniper. Distillers experiment with unconventional ingredients to create unique, contemporary profiles. This approach reflects a tendency to push the traditional boundaries of gin, giving rise to a wide variety of spirits.

Yellow gin

This term refers to more complex, barrel-aged gins, acquiring a yellow hue and woody tones.

SLOE GIN

Traditionally made by macerating sloes in gin, imparting a natural sweetness and rich berry aromas. This fruity, slightly sweet liqueur can also be made with other types of berries.

NAVY STRENGTH GIN

Prized in the UK, gin was authorized in limited quantities on Royal Navy ships but was often of mediocre quality due to its dilution. Officers tested its purity using gunpowder, similar to the "Gunpowder proof" test for rum. Navy Strength gins, which must contain at least 57% alcohol, evoke these spirits historically carried on Royal Navy ships.

OLD TOM GIN

This takes its name from an 18th-century British legend. According to tradition, bars illegally sold gin under the guise of a black cat sign, "Old Tom," which became a recognizable symbol. Customers would insert money into a slot under the sign and receive gin through a hidden tube, simulating the cat's "paw," thus circumventing the strict liquor laws of the day. This gin, a cross between genever and London Dry, is distinguished by a smoother profile due to a slight addition of sugar after distillation.

BATHTUB GIN

Despite its name, it is not made in a bathtub but rather takes its name from the makeshift methods used for its clandestine production during Prohibition. This bootleg gin was produced by mixing counterfeit alcohol with juniper oil or other plants to imitate the taste of the original gin, often without distillation. Bathtubs, used to mix the ingredients, symbolize this era. Today, it's used with a touch of nostalgia to evoke the spirit of resourcefulness and resistance during Prohibition.

PINK GIN

Popular in England in the 19th century, Pink Gin, so named for the pinkish hue added by Angostura, is enjoying a resurgence today. Modern distilleries make more complex versions with elaborate aromatics. With its herbal, spicy, and citrus notes, it lends a unique complexity to cocktails and pairs well with a variety of ingredients.

ARCHDUCHESS

EQUIPMENT

GLASS TYPE: FLUTE

INGREDIENTS:

- 1⅓ fl oz (40 ml) botanical gin with gentian, or an English distilled gin
- ⅔ fl oz (20 ml) lemon juice
- ⅔ fl oz (20 ml) cane syrup (Monin)
- BEER: Berliner Weisse red fruits (Grand Duc Brewery)
- 1 raspberry
- 1 sugar tuile
- Ice

IN THE SHAKER

1 – Pour all ingredients except beer and garnishes into shaker, then fill with ice and shake.
2 – Serve through a double strainer.
3 – Top with beer, stir.
4 – Garnish: one raspberry and a sugar tuile.

Citrus juice

The use of citrus juices brings key benefits to cocktails:

1. BALANCE OF FLAVORS

- **Acidity:** the acidity of juices such as lemon or lime is essential as it balances the sweetness of syrups and liqueurs with the strength of alcohol.
- **Complexity**: the acidity of citrus adds complexity and enhances the flavors of cocktails.

2. FRESHNESS AND AROMA

- **Freshness:** they give a feeling of freshness, ideal for summer cocktails or refreshing drinks.
- **Flavors:** each citrus fruit has a distinct profile: lemon and lime for zesty freshness, orange and grapefruit for fruity sweetness.

3. VISUAL AND SENSORY APPEAL

- **Color:** citrus juices color cocktails, making them visually appealing.
- **Texture:** some juices, such as grapefruit juice, can be slightly creamy.
- **Cloudy appearance:** the pulp and natural particles of citrus juices can cloud cocktails. This cloudiness is attractive and indicates the freshness and naturalness of the juice.
- **Lemon juice:** adds a crisp, clean acidity.
- **Lime juice:** gives a sharper acidity and a distinct aroma.
- **Orange juice:** its natural sweetness suits fruitier, less acidic cocktails.
- **Grapefruit juice:** offers a unique bitterness and subtle sweetness.

Fruit juices

They play a crucial role in mixology, giving flavor, color, and texture to cocktails. They add sweetness, freshness or balance acidity, and bitterness.

Available pure, concentrated, in nectar, purée, or homemade, juices offer a varied palette to personalize every cocktail. The quality and type of juice chosen greatly impact the overall cocktail.

100% PURE JUICE

Characteristics: made directly from fresh fruit, with no added sugar, water, or preservatives.

Advantages: offers an authentic and natural fruit taste, with superior quality and intensity of flavor, ideal for high-end cocktails that highlight the purity of the ingredients.

PURE JUICE

Characteristics: similar to 100% pure juice but may include water or added sugar.

Advantages: retains a natural taste and good quality, while being more affordable than 100% pure juice.

JUICE FROM CONCENTRATE

Characteristics: made by rehydrating concentrated juice, often with the addition of sugar and water.

Advantages: more economical, with a longer shelf life, this juice has a less natural taste than pure juice but is still practical for large-volume cocktails or on a limited budget.

FRUIT NECTARS

Characteristics: contains fruit juice, water, and quite a lot of sugar, with a consistency often thicker than that of juices.

Advantages: offers a rich texture, adding smoothness and creaminess to cocktails, ideal for creamy drinks or smoothies.

FRUIT PURÉE

Characteristics: made with whole blended fruits, these purées retain the pulp and fiber of the fruit.

Advantages: gives a dense texture and deep flavor, ideal for cocktails requiring a rich consistency and pronounced fruity taste.

JUICE AND HOMEMADE PURÉE

Characteristics: prepared fresh with whole fruit, filtered or unfiltered depending on the desired texture.

Advantages: maximizes freshness, quality, and flavor control; ideal for cocktails where originality and customization are key.

Each type of juice or purée offers a unique taste, texture, and appearance, enabling mixologists to develop a wide range of cocktails for different occasions and preferences.

Liqueurs and creams

Sweet, unfermented alcoholic beverages made by macerating or infusing plants, roots, seeds, fruits, or bark in an alcoholic base.

Unlike brandies, which are all distilled, only certain liqueurs, particularly those made from plants and seeds, are distilled.

Others, like cherry liqueurs, use brandies as a base. Their alcohol content ranges from 15% to 55%.

THE DIFFERENCE BETWEEN LIQUEURS AND CREAMS:

- **Liqueurs**: more alcoholic and less sweet (3½ oz/34 fl oz [100 g/l] minimum).
- **Creams:** lower alcohol content (15–25%), sweeter (9–14 oz/34 fl oz [250–400 g/l]), thicker consistency.

MAIN STYLES OF LIQUEURS:

- **Fruity:** such as orange or cherry liqueur.
- **Herbaceous/spicy:** such as chartreuse or aniseed liqueur.
- **Creams:** richer in aromas, such as mint or cocoa creams.

Used for their delicacy, smoothness, and creaminess, they offer a wide aromatic range of fruits, herbs, spices, and plants, enriching the complexity of cocktails. They play a significant role, either as the main ingredient or as a complement.

N'IMP'CHIMP

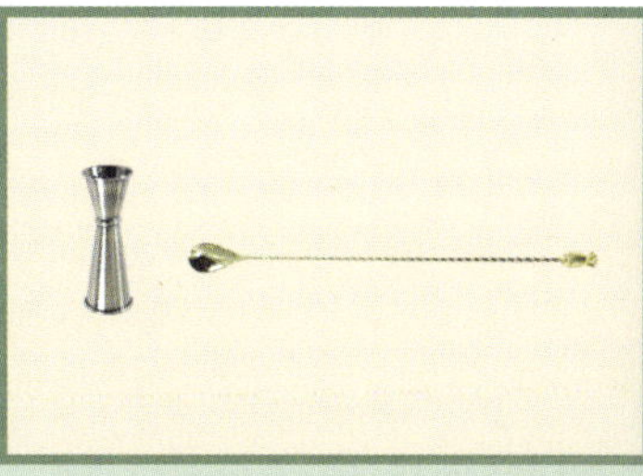

EQUIPMENT

GLASS TYPE: OLD FASHIONED

DID YOU KNOW? Banana cream appeared at the end of the 19th century with the boom in international trade, which made exotic fruits more accessible. Thanks to its distinctive aroma and natural sweetness, banana quickly became popular for infusion into spirits, particularly rum. This product was developed to meet the growing demand for fruity, exotic cocktails, particularly popular during Prohibition in the United States, where sweet flavors masked the taste of contraband spirits.

INGREDIENTS:

- 1⅓ fl oz (40 ml) Moonshine with notes of toasted grains
- ⅓ fl oz (10 ml) banana cream (Giffard)
- ⅓ fl oz (10 ml) yellow banana syrup (Monin)
- 1 dash Angostura cocoa
- BEER: Banana sour beer or a dry sour
- 2 slices dried banana
- 1 pansy
- 1 ice cube

BUILD IN THE GLASS

1 – Place an ice cube in the glass.
2 – Stir in all ingredients except beer and garnishes.
3 – Top with beer, stir.
4 – Garnish: two slices of dried banana and a pansy.

Egg

Some cocktails include fresh, uncooked chicken eggs, using the yolk, white, or both to add a creamy texture, rich consistency, and delicate foam. Here's how eggs are used in cocktails.

EGG WHITE

Used as an emulsifier, notably to give a frothy texture and a velvety mouthfeel. Often added to sour cocktails, a single egg white is enough for a cocktail.

EGG YOLK

Less common than egg white, it enriches certain cocktails, such as flips, giving them a rich, creamy texture and a slightly buttery flavor. One yolk is enough per cocktail.

WHOLE EGG

Some cocktails use whole eggs to optimize texture, complexity, and foam.

TEMPERATURE

For a better emulsion, use a room-temperature egg rather than a cold one. White proteins are more fluid at this temperature, making emulsification easier. A cold egg can delay the process and make it difficult to incorporate evenly. Allowing the egg to reach room temperature before use ensures a more consistent texture in the cocktail.

Tip: Do not crack the egg on the edge of the shaker to avoid introducing shell or salmonella. Break it on a flat surface to minimize this risk.

FRESH NOG'N'ALE

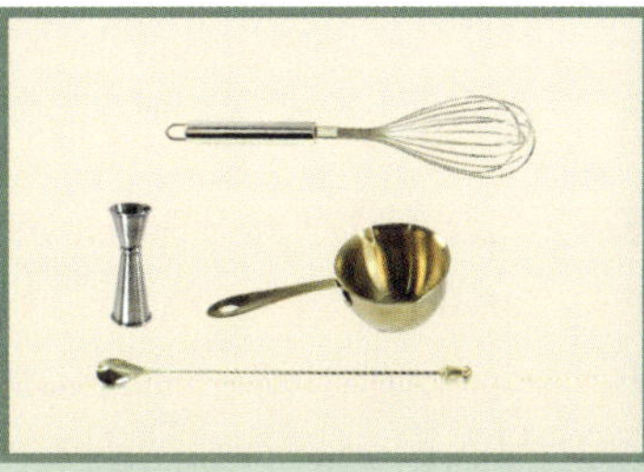

EQUIPMENT

GLASS TYPE: TODDY OR CUP

DID YOU KNOW? For centuries, eggs have been used in cocktails for their ability to create a creamy texture and stabilize mixtures. They symbolized wealth and added nutritional value to these refined drinks.

INGREDIENTS:

- 1⅓ fl oz (40 ml) Scotch whisky
- ⅓ fl oz (10 ml) red Vermouth (Le Nar)
- 4 fl oz (120 ml) of milk
- BEER: triple type
- A dash of Angostura cocoa bitters
- 1 egg
- Nutmeg
- Star anise

BUILD IN THE GLASS

1 – In a bowl, beat the egg with the sugar until frothy.

2 – Slowly pour cold milk into egg mixture while continuing to whisk.

3 – Add the whisky, Vermouth, Angostura cocoa bitters and a little beer.

4 – Stir gently to combine and pour into glass, topping with beer.

5 – Garnish: grate a little nutmeg and add a little star anise.

Rum

Centuries ago, in the Caribbean waters, in the heart of the sugar cane plantations, an age-old tradition was born – rum.

Steeped in the history of colonialism and slavery, this spirit crossed the oceans. The sugarcane boom began in the 15th century with the Portuguese and Spanish on islands such as Madeira and the Canary Islands, and spread to new colonies in the Americas, notably Haiti and Brazil. From 1630 onwards, the English and French expanded this crop to the West Indies.

Rum became a key part of the colonial economy, playing a crucial role in the triangular trade between Europe, Africa, and the Americas. Today, this colonial history still shapes rum production, and many producers celebrate this past through their traditions and manufacturing techniques.

The alcohol content of rum varies from 37.5% in Europe to 40% in the USA, although some may be stronger. Pure cane rum is produced exclusively in sugarcane-producing countries. Leading producers offer unique variations based on their manufacturing methods, ingredients, local traditions, and terroir.

It's one of the most widely produced alcoholic beverages. It's made from the fermentation and distillation of aged sugarcane or molasses juice. All rums, regardless of style or origin, are derived from sugar cane. They offer notes of cane sugar, vanilla, and spices. Different styles of rum enrich the variety of cocktails.

They are classified into three traditional families.

ENGLISH TRADITION (RUM)

The history of rum is closely linked to the British Navy which historically imported a variety of spirits without severe restrictions, since rum did not compete with the empire's local production. This enabled the English to export their Navy Rum or Tot/Pusser's Rum in large quantities to their colonies in the English-speaking Caribbean, Australia, and America, including destinations such as New England, Jamaica, and the Bahamas.

These rums, mostly made from molasses (around 90%) or occasionally from fresh cane juice, are renowned for their richness and strength. Their spicy sweetness and deep aromas vary according to the distillation and aging methods and techniques specific to each region. Aged in charred oak barrels that previously contained bourbon, these English rums develop intense aromas of vanilla, caramel, and wood, with a soft, velvety, spicy, and sweet texture, giving them a heavy, oily consistency.

Their sweetness makes them versatile, suitable for drinking neat, on the rocks, or in cocktails. They play an important role in Caribbean culture and are appreciated by rum lovers around the world.

DID YOU KNOW?

The term "Tot" refers to an old Royal Navy tradition dating back to the 17th century. To purify the drinking water in the holds, which deteriorated with the heat and humidity, from 1655 sailors were entitled to a daily ration of 500 ml of rum, called "The Daily Tot," a blend of rums from the British colonies. This tradition came to an abrupt end on July 31, 1970, known as "Black Tot Day," after a debate in the House of Lords on the problems caused by sailors' drunkenness and the introduction of computers on ships.

Have you heard of the Gunpowder Test? The term "Gunpowder proof" refers to a test carried out to check whether the sailors' rum had been diluted. Rum at around 55% strength would ignite when mixed with a small pile of gunpowder and lit, proving it hadn't been watered down. This test was crucial to ensure the quality of the gunpowder on board and the ship's armament. Saltpeter, a major component of black powder, does not dissolve well in pure alcohol but does dissolve well in water, allowing gunners to check the integrity of their gunpowder.

If high-quality gunpowder was soaked in overproof rum and then dried, it would ignite when lit. The high saltpeter content prevented the powder grains from dissolving into a non-flammable black sludge. However, poor-quality powder dissolved on contact with rum, leaving behind non-combustible soot. This "Gunpowder Test" led to the Navy's use of "overproof" rum to guarantee the quality of gunpowder. Rum that was too diluted dissolved the gunpowder due to its higher water content.

GROG

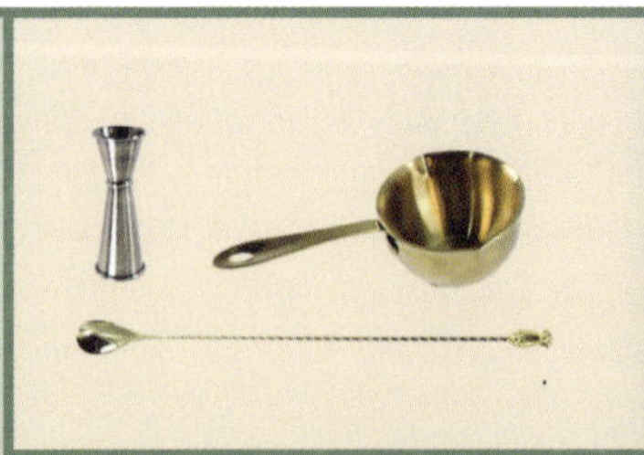

EQUIPMENT

GLASS TYPE: TODDY MUG OR CUP

DID YOU KNOW? Grog (rum toddy) gets its name from Admiral Edward Vernon, nicknamed "Old Grog" for his grogram cape. To combat alcoholism among his men and prevent diseases such as scurvy, he replaced the weak beer in the Royal Navy with rum diluted with water and lemon juice. This measure, initially unpopular, became a cherished naval tradition, with sailors raising their glasses in honor of Old Grog. Thus "grog" was born, a tradition that continues to this day.

INGREDIENTS:

- 1⅓ fl oz (40 ml) spiced dark rum (Botafago)
- 1 fl oz (30 ml) calvados (Avallen)
- ⅔ fl oz (20 ml) maple syrup (Monin)
- ⅓ fl oz (10 ml) cinnamon syrup (Monin)
- BEER: Wheat Wine Le Lascar (La Parisienne Brewery)
- Caramelized apples (optional)
- Spices: cinnamon, cloves, ginger, plus extra for garnish
- 1 candied orange slice

BUILD IN THE GLASS

1 – Caramelize apple wedges in saucepan, set aside (optional).
2 – Heat the beer without boiling in a saucepan with the spices for a few minutes to allow the flavors to infuse.
3 – Add a tablespoon of maple syrup to the glass, a little cinnamon syrup, caramelized apples and the spirits.
4 – Add the hot beer and stir.
5 – Garnish: a slice of candied orange and some spices.

SPANISH TRADITION (RUM)

The Spanish colonies, including Cuba, the Dominican Republic, Puerto Rico, and others, have had a profound influence on the world of rum. This Hispanic tradition continues, with the production of rums in Europe, particularly in Andalusia, the Canary Islands, and Madeira.

They are produced almost exclusively from molasses (>95%) or cane honey, a thick syrup made from the first pressing of the juice. Light and delicate, these rums are distinguished by their sweetness, roundness, and subtle aromas. Often aged in American bourbon oak barrels, they offer notes of vanilla, caramel, and wood. Their natural sweetness makes them versatile, whether enjoyed neat or in cocktails. It should be noted that there are rums made from fresh cane juice, particularly in regions producing agricultural rum, such as the Dominican Republic and Puerto Rico. They range from light, like those from Cuba, to premium, such as those from Guatemala or Panama, offering a complex palette that includes floral and fruity notes.

The Cuban style of rum features aguardiente, essential to this tradition. After mastering the distillation of light rums, Cubans returned to ancestral methods to produce rich and powerful aguardientes. These spirits are often blended with lighter rums to create a delicate balance, combining intensity and sweetness.

The spirit 'aguardiente', translated from Spanish as 'fiery water', illustrates its high alcohol content, generally between 29% and 60%, varying according to country and production method. Traditionally distilled in several Spanish-speaking countries, including Spain and Latin America, aguardiente is often made from fermented sugarcane juice. However, some make it from other ingredients such as corn, grapes, or apples. Central to Spanish-speaking traditions, it is deeply rooted in the cultural heritage of the regions where it is produced.

Have you heard of the Solera method? Often used for rum and sherry, this method involves stacking the casks in different layers, with the oldest at the bottom and the youngest on top. During the aging process, some of the contents of the oldest casks are removed for bottling, and these casks are then topped up with the contents of the casks immediately above, creating a continuity in the blending of generations. This process ensures a homogeneous blend and enhances the complexity of the final product.

FRENCH TRADITION (RUM)

The history of French rum is linked to colonial expansion in the Caribbean and Indian Ocean. The main rum-producing regions are the French West Indies, including Martinique, Guadeloupe, Marie-Galante, and Saint-Barthélemy, as well as French Guiana and the Indian Ocean, particularly Reunion and Mauritius. These territories, which are major centers of sugar cane production, have seen rum become a major industry, stimulating the local economy and culture.

Guadeloupe and Martinique, in particular, were at the heart of France's lucrative sugar trade. Their expertise in distillation on the mainland led them to favor sugarcane plantations, marking the beginning of the history of rum, an era shared with the English on the neighboring islands.

French agricultural rums, distilled from vesou (fresh sugarcane juice), retain the freshness and delicate aromas of sugarcane, offering fine, highly aromatic profiles, with tones of banana and citrus, enriching their taste complexity.

Tequila

Tequila, originally from Jalisco, Mexico, has evolved since pre-Hispanic times. Indigenous peoples fermented agave juice to create "pulque." The arrival of the Spanish in the 16th century introduced distillation, transforming pulque into tequila.

It's a Mexican spirit distilled with at least 51% blue agave, harvested at maturity (eight to 12 years). The hearts of the agaves, called "piñas," are cooked and crushed to extract the juice. This fermented juice is distilled twice to concentrate the alcohol. Depending on the variety (blanco, reposado, añejo), tequila may be aged in oak barrels. Its alcohol content ranges from 35% to 55%.

There are several types of tequila:

- **Blanco (or silver):** unaged (less than two months), clear, capturing the sweet flavor of agave.
- **Reposado**: aged in oak barrels for two months to a year, offering a balance of agave and woody notes.

- **Añejo:** aged longer (one to three years), it has a richer, more complex flavor.
- **Extra añejo:** aged over three years, very rich and complex.

MEZCAL

Originally from Mexico, mezcal was traditionally drunk in southern regions such as Oaxaca.

Mezcal, like tequila, emerged from the fermentation and distillation techniques of the Spanish conquistadors. Distilled from a variety of agaves, it is distinguished by its smoky taste, yet its alcohol content is similar to that of tequila.

Various agaves, often wild and ripe between seven to 30 years, are cooked in earth-covered pits, giving the mezcal its distinctive smoky note. The cooked piñas are crushed, the juice fermented and distilled, sometimes with the fibers, in traditional stills.

The main difference is the type of agave used and the production process. Traditionally smoked mezcal is distilled with various agaves.

There are various types of mezcal:

- **Joven:** unaged, clear, retains the pure, smoky character of agave.
- **Reposado and añejo:** similar to tequila, they are aged for at least a year in casks and develop sweeter, more complex flavors.

Tequila and mezcal, two distinct expressions of Mexican culture, reflect the diversity of the distillation tradition.

Tequila brings freshness and a lively, smooth profile, while mezcal offers smoky tones.

ESPRESSO MARTINI SWING

EQUIPMENT

GLASS TYPE: MARTINI

DID YOU KNOW? The name "espresso martini" comes from the glass in which the cocktail is served, similar to that of a martini. However, contrary to popular belief, the espresso martini recipe does not contain martini, but rather vodka, coffee liqueur and espresso, which can sometimes be confusing.

INGREDIENTS:

- 1⅓ fl oz (40 ml) Mezcal Joven (Lokita)
- ⅓ fl oz (10 ml) coffee liqueur (Ninebar)
- ⅓ fl oz (10 ml) coffee syrup (Monin)
- 1 espresso
- BEER: Rattle & Rum (Brewdog Brewery)
- 1 gold leaf
- Coffee beans
- Ice

IN THE SHAKER

1 - Add all ingredients except beer and garnishes to shaker, fill with ice and shake.
2 - Serve through a double strainer.
3 - Top with beer, stir.
4 - Garnish: a gold leaf and a few coffee beans.

Triple sec

This clear, sweet French orange liqueur is made from dried orange peel, giving it a citrusy note. Triple sec refers to the triple distillation of orange peel to produce a refined liqueur with an alcohol content ranging from 25 to 40%. Some orange liqueurs made with triple sec, such as Grand Marnier and Dry Curaçao, add cognac and brandy, using curaçao bitter orange peel for a unique flavor, regardless of color. Essential in many classic cocktails, it adds sweetness, orange flavor, and depth without overpowering the rest. Distinct and versatile, it has an unmistakable profile in mixology and balances drinks by offering a citrus sweetness and a pronounced orange tone to cocktails.

DANDY WAR'ALE

EQUIPMENT

GLASS TYPE: TASTING

DID YOU KNOW? Although triple sec is often associated with France, its origins date back to 19th-century Netherlands. It is derived from curaçao, an orange liqueur made from the peel of bitter oranges grown on the island of Curaçao, a Dutch colony off the coast of Venezuela.

INGREDIENTS:

- 1⅓ fl oz (40 ml) brandy (Mr Gaston)
- ⅔ fl oz (20 ml) triple sec (Denoix)
- ⅔ fl oz (20 ml) verbena liqueur
- BEER: a sour with thyme or a classic sour
- Lemon peel
- 1 snapdragon
- Ice

IN THE SHAKER

1 – Pour all ingredients except beer and garnishes into shaker, fill with ice and shake.
2 – Serve through a double strainer.
3 – Top with beer, stir.
4 – Garnish: lemon peel and a snapdragon.

Syrups

Syrups are sweet solutions used in cocktails to add sweetness, flavor, and sometimes color. They are generally made from a mixture of sugar and water, sometimes infused with herbs, spices, fruit, or flavoring.

MAKING HOMEMADE SYRUP

To make a simple syrup, you can use two methods: hot (fast) or cold (slow). The hot method is faster, but the cold method better preserves the delicate flavors.

- **Hot:** mix equal parts of water and sugar, heat until dissolved, leave to cool.
- **Cold:** mix equal parts of water and sugar, stirring until the sugar dissolves.
- **Flavored syrup:** add citrus zest, herbs or spices during heating to infuse flavors. Store in a clean, airtight container in the refrigerator for about one month
- **Honey syrup:** mix equal parts of honey and water, heat gently to dissolve. For a thicker consistency, increase the proportion of honey. For example, three parts honey to one part water will produce a richer syrup. Adjust proportions to taste.
- **Ginger syrup:** Boil water, sugar and slices of fresh ginger for a spicy syrup.
- **Lavender syrup:** infuse dried lavender flowers in a simple syrup for a soothing, floral touch.
- **Cinnamon syrup:** boil cinnamon sticks, water and sugar for a spicy, comforting syrup.
- **Chili syrup:** add fresh or dried chilies to a simple syrup for a spicy, bold twist.
- **Basil syrup:** infuse fresh basil leaves in a simple syrup for a fresh, herbaceous touch

Sodas

Sodas are non-alcoholic, carbonated, sweetened and flavored drinks. There is a wide variety available, each with its own characteristics.

- **Sparkling mineral waters:** rich in minerals, sometimes salty, ideal for preserving the aromatic profile of spirits, they offer a subtle effervescence without altering the cocktail's flavors.

- **Seltzer:** provides the perfect carbonation to increase cocktail volume, while maintaining flavor balance.
- **Ginger ale:** offers a light sweetness and a subtle note of ginger, ideal for sweetening cocktails and adding a spicy touch.
- **Ginger beer:** more pronounced than ginger ale, it offers spiciness and a robust ginger note.
- **Tonic:** sometimes flavored, it adds the characteristic bitterness of quinine and a subtle sweetness.
- **Soda water or club soda:** very fizzy, similar to seltzer but sometimes with a hint of minerality, it increases the volume of the cocktail without really altering the flavor. Each type of soda plays a unique role, adding effervescence, sweetness, specific flavor, or balancing the other components.

PAMPLO-MANGO

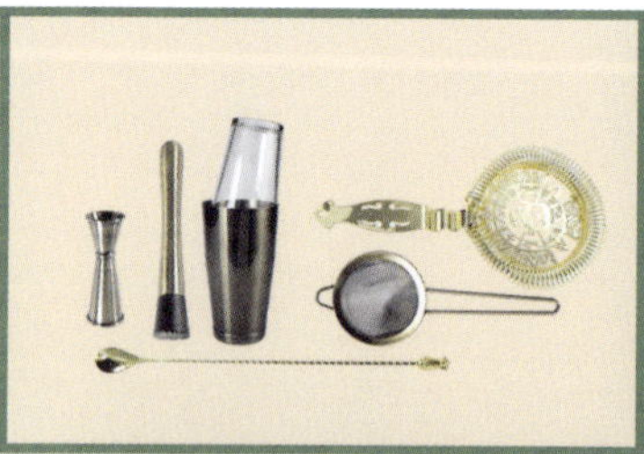

GLASS TYPE: FLUTE

INGREDIENTS:

- ⅔ fl oz (20 ml) alcohol-free, floral, spicy, peppery gin
- ⅓ fl oz (10 ml) lemongrass syrup (Monin)
- A few pieces of mango (or 1 fl oz [30 ml] juice)
- 1⅓ fl oz (40 ml) lemonade
- ⅔ fl oz (20 ml) pineapple syrup (Monin)
- BEER: Alcohol-free IPA (Vanderstreek Brewery)
- Ice

IN THE SHAKER

1 – Reserving some for garnish, crush the mango pieces and pour in all the ingredients except the beer.
2 – Fill shaker with ice and shake.
3 – Serve over ice, double filtered.
4 – Top with beer, stir.
5 – Garnish: a mango fan.

Fortified wines

In the 17th century, the English discovered Portuguese wine after an embargo on their favorite wine, Bordeaux claret. The Treaty of Methuen in 1703 promoted trade, allowing the English to establish trading houses in Portugal in exchange for reduced taxes on Portuguese wine, which was fortified with brandy to better withstand sea travel.

The English merchant Jean Beardsley increased the alcohol content of port, creating the modern version enjoyed in Europe today.

With an alcohol content of between 15 and 22%, these wines are fortified with alcohol (often brandy), increasing the alcohol content and stopping fermentation to preserve some of the natural sugar. Unlike A.B.V.s (alcohol by volume), they contain no additives, sugar, herbs, or spices. They offer fruity, nutty, and often sweet notes, ideal for sophisticated cocktails.

There are three main types of fortified wines.

1. PORT

Originating in Portugal's Douro Valley, Port was exported to the Portuguese colonies of Cape Verde, Madeira, Brazil, and the Azores, and especially to England for its colonies, under specific trade agreements.

There are two main categories of Port: those aged reductively, starting in casks and finishing in bottles, and those aged oxidatively in oak barrels.

REDUCTIVE

Aged in airtight tanks, unlike oxidative Ports, preserving their intense color and fruity aromas. Bottled two years after harvest, it continues aging in the bottle.

- **Ruby:** young and fruity, this blend of young wines aged for about three years in casks has a deep red color and lively red fruit aromas. The blending, after selection of the best wines, produces the "Fine Ruby" and "Ruby Reserve" versions. On the palate, it is soft, fruity, and less complex than the Tawny.
- **LBV (Late Bottled Vintage):** a style close to vintage, first aged four to six years in barrels, then in bottles. As a vintage-dated wine, it offers a deep color and rich tannins, while being less full-bodied than a classic Vintage Port.
- **Vintage:** made with grapes from a single exceptional year and from a single harvest, it is considered to be of superior quality by the winemaker and approved by the Port Wine Institute. After two years in casks, it is aged in bottles, defined by its strength and richness, reaching its peak after about ten years.

OXIDATIVE

Barrel aging encourages oxidation, creating interactions between the wine, air and wood, giving the wine its purple or mahogany hue.

- **White:** made from white grape varieties, it matures for two to three years in barrels or vats, before being bottled. The age references 10, 20, 30, and over 40 years reflect its character. It has a soft, aromatic palette, ranging from citrus to nuts, flowers and sometimes sweet spices and vanilla, varying according to the aging process.
- **Tawny:** aged in barrels for at least three years, these fortified wines have a tufted topaz color, hence their English name.
- **Tawny "Reserve":** made from blends aged for at least six years and certified as superior quality, it often offers notes of dried fruits, red berries, and spices.
- **Tawny "Age Statement":** a blend of several vintages – 10, 20, 30, or even over 40 years old – it displays a deep amber hue and reveals a complex bouquet of tobacco, leather, dried fruits, chocolate, and oak.
- **Colheitas:** a Port with a dark golden color and refined aromas of tobacco, ripe fruit, cooked fruit, vanilla, and nuts. From a single exceptional harvest, aged in barrels for at least seven years, it has incredible aging potential. The bottling date, indicated on the label, attests to its long maturation, characterized by remarkable finesse.

2. MADEIRA

From the island of Madeira, renowned for its unique heating process called "estufagem," Madeira offers distinct tones of walnut, candied fruit, and caramel. Production began in the 15th century, when the island became a major stopover for ships bound for the New World, the west coast of Africa, or the Indies.

Types: dry, semi-dry, sweet, depending on the grape variety used.

3. SHERRY

Originating from the Jerez region of Spain, sherry's popularity grew during colonization, especially in the 16th century. Trade with the colonies stimulated demand for this wine. The solera aging system was perfected, contributing to its unique profile and ability to age well, crucial for long sea journeys.

Types: Fino (dry and light), Oloroso (darker and richer).

PORTO BACK FLIP

GLASS TYPE: TASTING

DID YOU KNOW? The egg yolk adds a velvety texture and natural sweetness, balancing the whisky and beer tones for a richer taste experience.

INGREDIENTS:

- 1⅓ fl oz (40 ml) Maker's Mark whisky
- 1⅓ fl oz (40 ml) 10-year-old red Port (Valdouro)
- ⅓ fl oz (10 ml) salted caramel syrup (Monin)
- BEER: an IGA-style beer: Italian Grape Ale (beer brewed with grape must)
- 1 egg yolk
- Nutmeg powder
- Ice

IN THE SHAKER

1 – In the shaker, add all the ingredients except the beer and nutmeg, and do an initial dry shake.
2 – Fill with ice, then shake it again.
3 – Serve through a double strainer.
4 – Top with beer, stir.
5 – Garnish: sprinkle with nutmeg.

Vodka

Its history is rooted in the agricultural traditions of Eastern Europe, becoming the national spirit of many countries that once belonged to the Russian Empire: Poland, Ukraine, Finland. It developed locally in these regions, reflecting the use of available agricultural products such as potatoes, beets, and grains. Its popularity then spread worldwide, but it remains closely associated with its Russian and Polish roots.

A spirit distilled from grain, grapes, potatoes, or beet, vodka is often made with a single ingredient, usually wheat.

Vodka generally contains around 40% alcohol, the minimum requirement being 37.5%.

Here are the various families:

STANDARD-NEUTRAL

These vodkas aim for a clean, pure taste, with little or no tones other than that of the alcohol itself. They are often used in cocktails where you don't want the alcohol to dominate the other ingredients. This is the most common form of vodka.

FLAVORED

Infused with fruit, herb, or spice flavors, these vodkas add a distinctive aromatic dimension to cocktails without the need for additional ingredients.

PREMIUM-COMPLEX

Often artisanal or premium (careful distillation methods, attention to detail at every stage, use of premium ingredients), they aim to create subtle, distinctive flavors, derived from the type of grain or other ingredients, for superior purity and smoothness.

Perfect for balanced cocktails, this vodka type enhances the other ingredients, adding alcohol without weighing down the cocktail's profile.

THE BEER LEBOWSKI

EQUIPMENT

GLASS TYPE: METAL TUMBLER

DID YOU KNOW? The name "White Russian" refers to the cocktail's white color and its vodka-based composition. "White" evokes the cream floating above the mix, while "Russian" alludes to vodka, a spirit traditionally associated with Russia. In this way, the name captures both the look and the key ingredients of the cocktail.

INGREDIENTS:

- 1 fl oz (30 ml) Koskenkorva vodka
- ½ fl oz (15 ml) vanilla-hazelnut liqueur (La Capricieuse)
- ⅔ fl oz (20 ml) skim milk
- BEER: French Toast Banger (Pohjala Brewery)
- 1 chocolate-vanilla wafer
- Ice

IN THE SHAKER

1 – In the shaker, add all the ingredients except the beer and wafer and do an initial dry shake.
2 – Fill with ice, then shake it again.
3 – Serve through a double strainer.
4 – Top with beer, stir.
5 – Garnish: a chocolate-vanilla wafer.

Whisky

The history of whisky goes back many centuries in Scotland and Ireland. Unlike rum and gin, this alcohol is not directly linked to colonization. Its popularity in Europe was influenced by global trade. In America, its expansion was mainly due to European immigration, particularly from Scotland and Ireland in the 17th and 18th centuries. Before their arrival, there was no whisky-making tradition in North America.

These immigrants adapted their methods to local ingredients like corn and rye, giving rise to unique American whisky styles like bourbon and rye whisky. Today's American whisky draws its essence from the expertise of newcomers from Europe.

It is distilled from fermented grain mash, particularly barley, aged in wooden barrels for at least three years. Its alcohol content is generally between 40% and 50%.

WHISKY

- **Single malt:** typically Scottish, made from malted barley and distilled in a single distillery, it is distinguished by its complexity and depth.
- **Grain whisky:** made from a variety of cereals, it is less complex, lighter, and sweeter.
- **Blended:** popular worldwide, readily available, made from a blend of single malt and grain whisky, it aims for a balanced, accessible profile.
- **Blended malt:** complex and nuanced, this is a blend of several single malts from different distilleries. No grain whisky is included.
- **Scotch:** the term "Scotch" refers to all types of whisky produced and aged in Scotland.
- **Single malt Scotch whisky:** distilled in a single distillery from malted barley only.
- **Blended Scotch whisky:** a blend of several single malts and grain whiskys from several distilleries.
- **Single grain Scotch whisky:** whisky from a single distillery that may include other grains in addition to malted barley.
- **Blended malt Scotch whisky:** a blend of several single malts from various distilleries, without grain whisky.

- **Single grain:** produced in a single distillery, single grain differs from blended whiskies from multiple sources. Despite its name, it's made with several types of grain, mainly corn or wheat, complemented by a little malted barley, which makes it smoother and lighter than single malt.

WHISKEY

Bourbon: this American whisky is distilled with at least 51% corn and aged in charred new oak barrels, giving it aromas of vanilla, caramel, sweet spices, and wood, often making it softer and rounder than other whiskies.
Rye whiskey: this American whisky, made from at least 51% rye, is also aged in oak barrels. It offers spicier tones from the rye, but also fruity and sometimes herbaceous notes. Rye whisky is generally drier and spicier than bourbon.

DID YOU KNOW?

The difference in spelling between "whisky" and "whiskey" has historical and linguistic roots. The addition of the Irish "e" to the spelling of "whiskey" in the 19th century was intended to distinguish it from Scotch whisky, then perceived as being of inferior quality. Irish producers wanted to highlight the superiority of their whisky. This spelling was also brought to America by Irish immigrants, influencing the use of the spelling "whiskey" in the USA.

In Scotland, Canada, Japan, and elsewhere, "whisky" without the "e" is maintained, reflecting regional tradition. This distinction serves to differentiate whisky styles and traditions between countries, highlighting their cultural and historical heritage.

HAZY HYPE OLD FASHIONED

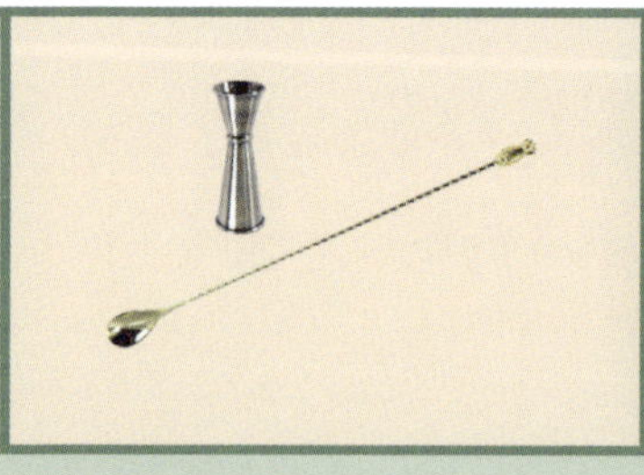

EQUIPMENT

GLASS TYPE: OLD FASHIONED

DID YOU KNOW? The term "Old Fashioned" appeared in the early 19th century to designate simple, traditional cocktails, in contrast to the more elaborate creations of the time. The term has become an umbrella term to describe classic, timeless cocktails. The "Old Fashioned" or whisky glass, often used to serve this style of cocktail, bears the same name because of this association with simplicity.

INGREDIENTS:

- 1⅓ fl oz (40 ml) Redemption whisky
- 1 fl oz (30 ml) Gentiana Amaro
- 1 fl oz (30 ml) white vermouth (Berto)
- ⅓ fl oz (10 ml) chestnut syrup (Monin)
- BEER: a sour beer, preferably pineapple lime, otherwise a classic sour beer.
- Grapefruit peel
- An ice cube

BUILD IN THE GLASS

1 – Place an ice cube in the glass, add all the ingredients except the beer and peel and stir.
2 – Top with beer, stir.
3 – Express (squeeze) the peel over the drink.
4 – Garnish: grapefruit peel, scalloped with scissors.

DECORATIVE GARNISHES BY CATEGORY

More than just decorative, garnishes transform drinks into unique experiences. Delicate fruit, fragrant citrus zest, flowers, or leaves enrich each glass visually and aromatically. Finishing touches such as rimming the glass or a sprinkling of cocoa add a creative touch, awakening the senses before the first sip. These details are not only decorative but also serve to complement and enrich the cocktail's flavor, affirming their essential role in the drink's composition.

Spicy

Spices are prized gems in the world of mixology. Their presence in cocktails transcends simple blends to create rich sensory experiences. Whether they add heat, depth, or an exotic touch, they add aromatic complexity, elevating each sip to the next level. They offer a unique sensation, revealing the rich aromas of each glass.

STAR ANISE

Delicately placed on top of a cocktail, star anise is an eye-catcher. Beyond its fragrant role, whole, ground, or in syrup form, it emits an enticing aroma, offering notes of aniseed freshness.

CINNAMON

Fragrant and versatile, cinnamon adds a warm autumnal touch to hot or cold cocktails, with spiced cider, coffee, hot chocolate, maple syrup, whisky, or rum. Whether ground or in sticks, it releases comforting aromas, harmoniously balancing each sip for a rich and complex experience.

CLOVE

Dried and fragrant, cloves add a rustic, spicy touch to hot or cold cocktails like mulled wine or refreshing drinks. Their intense fragrance releases enveloping essential oils, enriching the sensory experience.

LICORICE

With its powerful aniseed-like aroma, licorice adds a unique depth to cocktails, offering a harmony of sweetness, mild bitterness, woodiness and a subtle hint of spice. Its captivating fragrance combines perfectly with a variety of ingredients, opening up a whole range of creative possibilities for bartenders.

GINGER

This spicy, slightly sweet root, prized for its strong character, adds a noticeable warming sensation to cocktails. It offers a spicy heat and a slightly tangy exotic touch, balancing the sweetness of wood notes for a welcome complexity.

Suitable for a variety of beverages, with or without alcohol, its warming effect varies in intensity according to the quantity used, adding a subtle dynamic to mixtures.

PEPPER

Each pepper variety has its own distinct advantages. When ground, it offers an intense, fresh, and spicy flavor that varies in intensity depending on the amount used and the type of pepper.

Pepper syrup adds zest and aromatic power, prolonging the sensation on the palate. Infused in vodka or gin, it creates spicy bases for original cocktails, offering a dynamic and intriguing taste experience.

CHILI PEPPER

Often associated with intense heat, chili pepper is a dynamic ingredient for cocktails. Like pepper, there are many varieties, each with its own distinct flavor profile. Used as an infused syrup or in crushed pieces in a glass, it adds controlled, intense heat. Powdered or infused into spirits such as tequila, it creates a spicy base for chili pepper cocktails.

NUTMEG

Sweet and aromatic, nutmeg is used in powder form to add a delicate touch to cocktails. Freshly grated, it reveals hints of hazelnut and wood, adding a touch of elegance to the presentation. It is ideal in hot drinks such as rum toddy or spiced cider. Infused in spirits such as rum, it creates spicy bases, while in syrup it complements spiced punches. Used in hot winter drinks, it provides a comforting sensation.

VANILLA

Versatile vanilla finds its place in cocktails, offering a sweet, soothing aroma. In extract, syrup, or pod form, it releases sweet fragrances. Vanilla syrup sweetens and flavors cocktails like the vanilla whisky sour. Rum-infused pods add rich aromas. It can also be used to stir drinks or as a visual garnish.

THE INSOLENT

EQUIPMENT

GLASS TYPE: CHAMPAGNE COUPE

INGREDIENTS:

- 1⅓ fl oz (40 ml) gin (Kerr's)
- ⅓ fl oz (10 ml) ginger liqueur (The King's Ginger)
- ½ fl oz (15 ml) lemon juice
- ⅓ fl oz (10 ml) elderflower syrup (Monin)
- BEER: Blanche Lambicus (Timmerman Brewery)
- 1 small pinch pepper
- 1 slice ginger
- 1 rice flower
- Ice

IN THE SHAKER

1 – Pour all ingredients except beer and garnishes into shaker, then fill with ice and shake.
2 – Serve through a double strainer.
3 – Top with beer, stir.
4 – Garnish: a slice of ginger and a rice flower.

Fruity/citrus

CITRUS FRUITS

Versatile citrus fruits offer unique aromas. They can be used as slices, wedges, juices, infusions, zests, macerations, syrups, jams or juice or fruit ice cubes.

PEEL

Essential in mixology for its bright, refreshing flavors, peel adds complexity to cocktails and can be presented in a variety of ways. Crushing citrus peel releases essential oils. Infusing citrus peel into spirits creates aromatic bases for more complex cocktails.

ORANGE

Juicy, soft, slightly tart and sweet, used with or without the peel, oranges add attractive color to cocktails. Often found in tropical cocktails, oranges create an exotic touch. Floating in slices with the peel, it can add a slight bitterness. For an eye-catching effect, place a slice or wedge on the rim of the glass, or as a fruit skewer.

LEMON

Essential in cocktails, lemon's refreshingly acidic aromatic properties provide a natural acidity that balances sugar and enhances their complexity, especially in summer drinks. Lemon slices or peel are often used as a visual garnish for a touch of elegance.

GRAPEFRUIT

Prized for its intense bitterness and pinkish juice that colors cocktails, grapefruit adds a pleasant freshness and subtle acidity. Ideal for refreshing drinks or balancing sweet beverages, its essential oils offer a resinous aroma that adds depth and complexity, while its slices often serve as a striking garnish.

LIME

Often used for its freshness, lime offers a tart and tangy flavor, slightly more intense than lemon, with a hint of bitterness that makes it perfect for balancing sweet cocktails. The essential oils in its peel add a distinctive, floral aroma. It can be used zested, juiced, candied, or sliced.

CITRUS TWIST

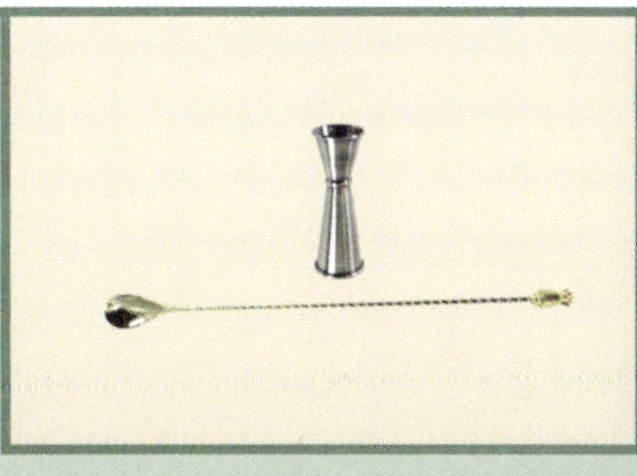

EQUIPMENT

GLASS TYPE: SLING

INGREDIENTS:

- ⅔ fl oz (20 ml) Cointreau
- ⅓ fl oz (10 ml) yuzu liqueur (Choya)
- ⅓ fl oz (10 ml) yuzu syrup (Bacanha)
- BEER: Tangerine Express Hazy IPA (Stone Brewery)
- 1 orange slice
- Ice

BUILD IN THE GLASS

1 – Fill the glass with ice and add all the ingredients except the beer and orange slice.

2 – Top with beer, stir.

3 – Garnish: a slice of orange.

Dairy

Historically, dairy products were commonly used in cocktails for their rich texture and sweetness, providing a contrast to strong spirits. Today, their use extends beyond cream and milk to include ingredients such as yoghurt, almond milk, and whipped cream. This development reflects the adaptation of mixology to contemporary food trends, transforming the sensory experience of cocktails. The integration of dairy products softens the acidity and balances the bitterness, creating harmony on the palate.

CONDENSED MILK

Dense and sweet, condensed milk is often used to add intense sweetness and thick texture to cocktails. Ideal for coffee and chocolate beverages, it gives them a richness and creaminess that transforms them into true liquid delights.

MILK

Milk lends a subtle sweetness and velvety texture to cocktails, balancing flavors and creating a harmonious mouthfeel. Its fluid consistency blends perfectly without weighing down the drink. Although it's often preferred for its creamy texture, other options such as almond or soy milk offer plant-based or low-fat alternatives. Each variety paves the way for innovative cocktails, offering new taste experiences.

WHIPPED CREAM

Whipped cream is a popular decorative element in cocktails. It adds a touch of sweetness and richness, transforming each sip into an indulgent experience. Used as a crowning touch, it goes very well with coffee or chocolate, bringing a contrasting lightness to the denser notes. It can also be flavored for added creativity.

VALHALL' ALE'NOG

EQUIPMENT

GLASS TYPE: TODDY CUP

DID YOU KNOW? Dairy products, such as milk and cream, have been classic ingredients in cocktails for centuries, offering a rich texture and natural sweetness that provide a velvety mouthfeel. Although their use is not new, they are enjoying a resurgence in popularity thanks to new trends in mixology, such as infused milk-based cocktails and artisanal flavored cream creations.

INGREDIENTS:

- 1 fl oz (30 ml) Bulleit bourbon
- ⅔ fl oz (20 ml) salted caramel syrup (Monin)
- 1 fl oz (30 ml) skim milk
- BEER: lightly smoked (Smoked Porter)
- Whipped cream
- Ice

IN THE SHAKER

1 – Place all ingredients except the beer and cream in the shaker and do an initial dry shake.
2 – Fill with ice, then shake it again.
3 – Serve through a double strainer.
4 – Top with beer, stir, add whipped cream.
5 – Garnish: whipped cream and a few grains of roasted malt.

Exotic fruits

Exotic fruits are a mixology staple, evoking sunshine and travel. They add tropical, fruity and often sweet notes, offering a wide variety of options for creating exotic, gourmet drinks.

MANGO

Fragrant, juicy and sweet, mango is a key ingredient in exotic cocktails. It adds natural sweetness, subtle acidity, and a creamy texture.

LYCHEE

Delicate, smooth, and juicy, lychee is popular in cocktails for its sweet and slightly tart flavor, as well as its floral and fruity notes reminiscent of muscat and rose.

BANANA

With its signature aroma, sweet taste, and smooth texture, the banana offers a pleasant sensory experience. Its distinctive sweet taste can help balance drinks or add a tropical note to cocktails.

FIG

This sweet fruit adds a refined touch thanks to its rich, smooth aroma and fleshy texture. Figs add a sweet, velvety dimension to cocktails, offering a sophisticated alternative to tantalize the taste buds of creative drink lovers.

PINEAPPLE

Often paired with rum, pineapple adds a tropical freshness and sweet-tart flavor, enhancing drinks with a bright, sun-kissed color.

PASSION FRUIT

Often used in cocktails, passion fruit offers a pleasant combination of sweetness and acidity, as well as a lovely exotic touch.

GUAVA

Guavas range in color from whitish to pinkish, depending on the variety, with a fragrant sweetness and a distinctive tropical note.

KIWI

Versatile in cocktails, the firm, juicy, and slightly grainy flesh of kiwi offers a tart and sweet flavor, as well as a touch of freshness. Its eye-catching green color adds originality.

COCONUT

Used in various forms in cocktails, coconut adds a creamy smoothness, sweetness, and tropical notes.

KIWI KICKER

EQUIPMENT

GLASS TYPE: TASTING

INGREDIENTS:

- 1 fl oz (30 ml) vodka (Berto)
- 1 fl oz (30 ml) (Agitator)
- A few pieces of ripe kiwi fruit (or 1⅓ fl oz [40 ml] juice)
- ⅓ fl oz (10 ml) kiwi syrup (Monin)
- ⅓ fl oz (10 ml) squeezed lemon juice
- 1 tbsp coconut cream
- BEER: One IPA (Oskar Blues Brewery)
- 1 kiwi slice
- Ice

IN THE SHAKER

1 – Mash a few pieces of kiwi, add the rest of the ingredients, except the beer and garnishes, and do an initial dry shake.
2 – Fill the shaker with ice and give it another shake.
3 – Serve through a double strainer.
4 – Top with beer, stir.
5 – Garnish: a slice of kiwi and pieces of dried mango.

Red & black fruits

Red and black fruits offer a rich palette of sweet and tart flavors, adding a lively and smooth dimension. Selected for their diverse taste profile, these dynamic fruits add a colorful touch and a unique sensory experience.

STRAWBERRY

Strawberries have a smooth, velvety texture that can sometimes be firm. Appreciated for their sweetness and slight acidity, they leave a pleasant, refreshing sensation. In cocktails, they add a bright red hue, offering an attractive visual aspect.

RASPBERRY

Raspberries color cocktails with a deep purplish red, adding visual appeal. They offer a velvety texture and whole seeds, adding delicacy. Their balance between sweetness and acidity brings a complexity of flavor and a distinctive fragrance, refining cocktails.

RED CURRANT

Depending on the variety, redcurrant berries range in color from yellow to deep red, almost purple, to pale pink and purple-black. Not very sweet, redcurrants have a bright, tart flavor depending on ripeness.

CRANBERRY

This brightly acidic red fruit imparts immediate freshness, perfect for balancing sweet flavors.

BLACKBERRY

Blackberries provide a sweetness and slight acidity that balance cocktails, adding freshness and a rounded finish. Their dark purple to red hue makes the drinks visually appealing.

BLUEBERRY

Blueberries are sweet and slightly tart and have a vibrant blue-violet color that adds a bluish touch to drinks, while providing natural antioxidants.

RASPBERRY BOUQUET

EQUIPMENT

GLASS TYPE: FLUTE

INGREDIENTS:

- 1 fl oz (30 ml) Amaretti (Lyre's)
- 1⅓ fl oz (40 ml) of non-alcoholic aperitif liqueur made from hibiscus flowers and plants
- A few strawberry pieces (or 1 fl oz [30 ml] juice)
- ⅓ fl oz (10 ml) hibiscus syrup (Monin)
- BEER: a non-alcoholic raspberry sour-style
- 1 candied hibiscus flower
- Ice

IN THE SHAKER

1 – Mash a few strawberry pieces, then add the rest of the ingredients except the beer and garnish.
2 – Fill shaker with ice and shake.
3 – Serve through a double strainer.
4 – Top with beer, stir.
5 – Garnish: a candied hibiscus flower.

Stone fruits

Rich in sweet and tart flavors, stone fruits add a vibrant, balanced touch to cocktails. Their juicy, fragrant flesh enriches drinks with a beautiful complexity, adding a fruity, gourmet dimension.

CHERRY

Juicy, tart, sweet, and tangy, this versatile fruit adds beautiful color and carefully enhances cocktails, balancing them or offering a deliciously fruity touch.

PEACH

The juiciness and sweetness of peaches add a natural freshness to cocktails, while its tender pulp offers a velvety texture. Its sweet, delicate taste is ideal for light beverages.

APRICOT

The apricot's creamy texture and sweet-tart flavor adds elegance to cocktails, while the juicy orange flesh adds a colorful, gourmet note.

PLUM

Sweet and tangy, plums offer a beautiful complexity. Their color ranges from deep red to almost black, adding a range of hues from pink to dark purple to drinks. They enrich cocktails with a velvety texture and aromatic depth, while giving them an appealing color.

BEERINI

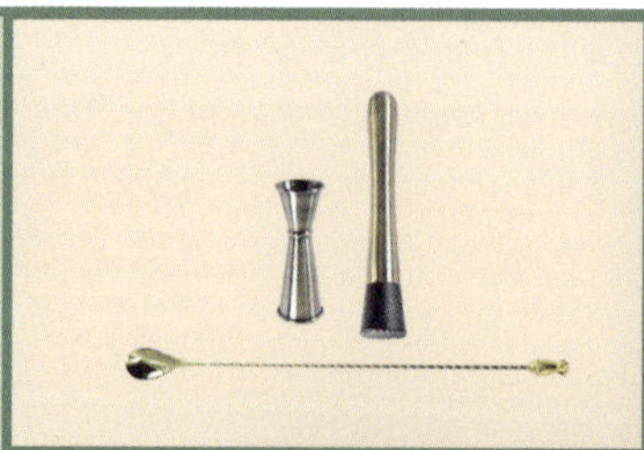

EQUIPMENT

GLASS TYPE: FLUTE

INGREDIENTS:

- ⅓ fl oz (10 ml) vine peach cream (Giffard)
- A few peach pieces (or 1⅓ fl oz [40 ml] juice)
- BEER: Pêcheresse (Lindemans Brewery)

BUILD IN THE GLASS

1 – Mash a few peach pieces into the mixing glass, reserving a segment for garnish.
2 – Place the peach juice and peach cream in the glass and stir.
3 – Top with beer, stir.
4 – Garnish: a peach segment roasted with a blowtorch (optional).

CELTIC PEAR SHANDY

EQUIPMENT

GLASS TYPE: TASTING

INGREDIENTS:

- 1 fl oz (30 ml) Classic whisky (Armorik)
- A few pear pieces (or 1⅓ fl oz [40 ml] juice)
- ⅔ fl oz (20 ml) lemon juice
- ⅓ fl oz (10 ml) gingerbread syrup (Monin)
- BEER: Ruby Ale XB (Theakston Brewery)
- Gingerbread

IN THE SHAKER

1 – Blend gingerbread and rim the glass with the gingerbread syrup and crumbs.
2 – Mash the pear pieces in the shaker.
3 – Add all ingredients except beer, leaving some pear pieces for garnish, fill with ice and shake.
4 – Serve through a double strainer.
5 – Top with beer, stir.
6 – Garnish: pear fan and gingerbread rim.

Seeded fruits

Seeded fruits offer a crunchy, juicy texture and a sweet, tangy flavor. Their versatility makes them ideal for a wide range of cocktails, adding freshness and complexity to drinks.

APPLE

Its crisp freshness and delicate acidity make apple a versatile ingredient in cocktails, providing a balanced taste experience. Its fresh juice blends harmoniously with spirits, adding a light fruitiness and subtle sweetness that is ideal for balancing alcoholic and non-alcoholic drinks.

PEAR

This delicate, juicy fruit offers sweetness and fragrance, harmoniously balancing cocktails. The sweet flavor and tender texture of pears enrich blends with a welcome natural sweetness.

GRAPE

Grapes offer a naturally sweet, slightly tart flavor that subtly refreshes drinks. Their hues range from pale green to deep red, enriching blends with a vibrant palette of colors.

Salty sea

These salty flavors evoke the very essence of the sea, offering a unique taste experience that transports connoisseurs to a refreshing realm of creativity. Their saline flavors and iodine aromas awaken the senses, adding a touch of the ocean to every sip.

OYSTER JUICE

Original and unusual in mixology, oyster juice offers an incredible salty and iodine flavor, adding a captivating depth to cocktails. Its delicate infusion reveals delicious coastal tones, creating a subtle balance between salty and umami.

SAMPHIRE

This crunchy-textured seaweed adds an original, salty touch to cocktails, creating a harmonious balance between earthy flavors and oceanic nuances. Its innovative use broadens the horizons of mixology by adding unexpected depth, evoking sea breezes and ocean expanses.

BLACK SEA WHISPER

EQUIPMENT

GLASS TYPE: LARGE COUPE

INGREDIENTS:

- 1⅓ fl oz (40 ml) Lower East Side Blended whisky
- ⅔ fl oz (20 ml) Antica Formula vermouth
- 1 fl oz (30 ml) oyster juice
- 1 tsp (5 ml) lemon juice
- ⅓ fl oz (10 ml) blueberry syrup (Monin)
- BEER: Imperial Stout with seaweed or classic
- 1 piece of dried seaweed
- Spherical lemon and vinegar beads
- Ice

IN A MIXING GLASS

1 – Open the oysters, collect the second juice and filter several times into a container. The advice against drinking water from an oyster refers to the first, very salty, water that comes out when the oyster is opened. Once it has been discarded, the oyster will produce a new juice that is much more enjoyable – this is the juice that should be kept.

2 – In mixing glass, add ice and all ingredients except beer and garnishes, stir.

3 – Serve through a double strainer.

4 – Top with beer, stir.

5 – Garnish: dried seaweed, spherical lemon and vinegar beads.

WHITE SEA WHISPER

EQUIPMENT

GLASS TYPE: MARTINI

INGREDIENTS:

- 1 fl oz (30 ml) Etsu Pacific gin
- ⅔ fl oz (20 ml) Lillet blanc
- ⅔ fl oz (20 ml) oyster juice
- 1 tsp (5 ml) lemon juice
- ⅓ fl oz (10 ml) lemon syrup (Monin)
- BEER: Gose style beer
- Lemon peel
- Samphire
- Ice

IN A MIXING GLASS

1 – Open the oysters, collect the second juice (see recipe page 89) and filter into a container several times.

2 – In mixing glass, add ice and all ingredients except beer and garnishes, stir.

3 – Serve through a double strainer.

4 – Top with beer, stir.

5 – Garnish: lemon peel and samphire.

Smoky

The addition of robust and complex smoky notes in unique ways, such as infusions from smokehouses, creates aromas that stimulate the sense of smell and a captivating, adventurous tasting experience.

GRILLED BACON

Grilled bacon, with its bold and distinctive flavor, enhances bourbon wood notes, offering a robust taste experience with sweet and salty flavors.

ROSEMARY SPRIG

Burnt resinous herbs add subtle smoke and herbaceous, woody notes to cocktails. Perfect with gin or vodka for a summery Mediterranean touch.

BBQ SAUCE

Using BBQ sauce in cocktails adds a unique combination of sweet, tangy, and smoky flavors, ideal with robust spirits such as whisky or mezcal, for a delicate balance between boldness and refinement.

SMOKED TEA

Smoked tea brings rich and complex aromas to cocktails. Its subtle woodiness and smoky notes make it an interesting ingredient, adding an intriguing dimension to original creations.

MARY'S HOT DOG

EQUIPMENT

GLASS TYPE: FANTASY

INGREDIENTS:

For the hot dog buns syrup:

- 1 sachet distiller's alpha-amylase enzyme (Rolling Beer)
- 17½ oz (500 g) hot dog buns
- 8½ fl oz (250 ml) of water

For the cocktail:

- 1 fl oz (30 ml) Woodford Reserve Bourbon
- ⅔ fl oz (20 ml) hot dog buns syrup
- 2 dashes of chipotle Tabasco
- BEER: Groteski (Iso-Kallas Brewery)
- 1 tsp BBQ sauce
- 1 chili pepper
- Ice

BUILD IN THE GLASS

1 – Blend the syrup ingredients until you get a paste.
2 – Transfer the paste into a vacuum-sealed bag and cook it in a water bath at 140°F (60°C) for two hours.
3 – Strain the mixture through a fine mesh straining bag. Reduce the liquid in a saucepan for a few minutes until it becomes a thick syrup.
4 – Add the bourbon, the BBQ sauce and the ice to the glass, top up with beer and stir.
5 – Add a few drops of chipotle Tabasco and stir.
6 – Garnish: a chili pepper.

Freshness

Freshness is crucial to many cocktails, bringing liveliness and brightness. Used creatively, it transforms an ordinary drink into a refreshing and dynamic experience.

MINT

A star in cooking and baking, mint is also a freshness champion in mixology, bringing essential freshness and liveliness to summer cocktails.

CUCUMBER

A refreshing vegetable, cucumber is perfect for summer drinks, offering a delicate, recognizable note that is fresh, subtle, and balanced in cocktails.

MELON

The ultimate symbol of summer, melon evokes sunny days and freshness. Its natural sweetness and juicy texture make it an ideal base for summer cocktails, bringing a refreshingly sweet note that everyone will enjoy.

GARDEN FRESH

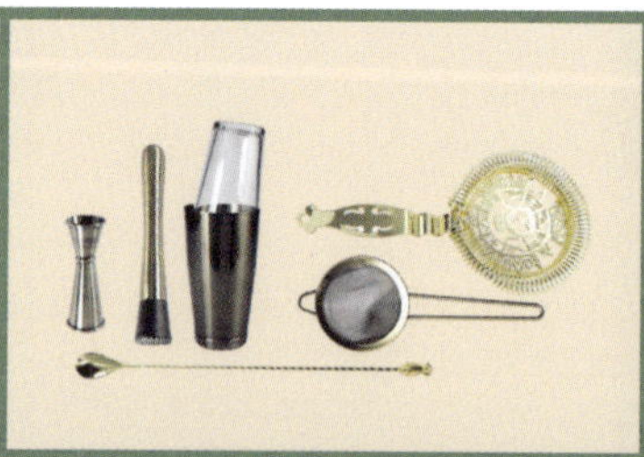

EQUIPMENT

GLASS TYPE: TASTING

INGREDIENTS:

- 1⅓ fl oz (40 ml) gin with spicy and floral notes
- 1 fl oz (30 ml) melon liqueur (Giffard)
- ⅓ fl oz (10 ml) cucumber syrup (Monin)
- A few pieces of melon (or 1⅓ fl oz [40 ml] melon juice)
- BEER: Blond Ale (not too bitter)
- 1 cube of melon
- 1 cucumber slice
- Mint leaves
- Ice

IN THE SHAKER

1 – Mash a few pieces of melon in a shaker, leaving a piece for garnish, then pour in all the ingredients except the beer and garnishes.
2 – Fill shaker with ice and shake.
3 – Serve through a double strainer.
4 – Top with beer, stir.
5 – Garnish: a cube of melon, a slice of cucumber and some mint leaves.

Vegetable and aromatic greenery

This category offers a variety of options for cocktails, from aromatic herbs to leaves and stems. Their presence brings freshness, originality, and a unique palette of aromas, allowing you to play with the complexity of flavors.

BASIL

This aromatic herb offers a unique sensory experience with its highly fragrant leaves, adding freshness and subtlety to cocktails. Its lightly peppery flavor enriches drinks with a refined palette, while its elegant appearance completes the presentation.

CELERY STALK

This thirst-quenching, modest but essential green stalk is a leading figure among the green elements in mixology, bringing freshness and crunch, for a refreshing and surprising sensory experience, while adding an elegant visual touch.

NETTLE

Often underestimated and perceived as a simple wild plant with unexpected potential, nettle surprises with its herbaceous freshness and earthy notes, adding a unique touch to cocktails with its fresh, peppery character.

THYME

A common seasoning, thyme brings a fragrant, intriguing note to the mix. Its delicate fragrance and earthy notes make it an aromatic herb prized for its freshness and versatility. Used as a garnish, infusion, or syrup, it adds a unique aromatic depth to beverages.

PROVENCIAL

EQUIPMENT

GLASS TYPE: OLD FASHIONED

INGREDIENTS:

- 1⅓ fl oz (40 ml) hop-infused gin
- ⅔ fl oz (20 ml) thyme liqueur (Bigallet)
- ⅔ fl oz (20 ml) squeezed lemon juice
- BEER: Sour with thyme or sour classic
- ½ fl oz (15 ml) honey
- 1 slice green melon, plus extra for garnish
- 1 bunch thyme, plus extra sprig
- Ice

IN THE SHAKER

1 – Dissolve the honey in a bowl with the lemon juice.

2 – Blend the melon with the thyme and strain.

3 – Pour all ingredients except beer and garnishes into the shaker, fill with ice, and shake.

4 – Serve over ice, double filtered.

5 – Top with beer, stir.

6 – Garnish: a slice of green melon and a sprig of thyme.

Woody

Beyond barrel-aged spirits, wood is emerging as an ingredient in its own right, imparting rustic tones and earthy, woody, and sometimes resinous aromas that enrich beverages and explore new dimensions. Whether through infusion, maceration, smoking, or artistic presentation, woody cocktails captivate the senses and expand the aromatic horizons of mixology.

PINE

Evoking the freshness of the forest, pine brings an authentic and original experience. Its needles, rich in essential oils, can be infused into syrups or liqueurs to distill woody and resinous aromas, while its branches infuse spirits with a subtle forest essence. A unique way to capture the raw beauty of nature in a cocktail.

JUNIPER

Its berries can be used fresh or dried to infuse spirits, while the branches are used for decoration, flavoring, or smoking cocktails. Its berries add woody, earthy, and spicy nuances, enriching cocktails with a unique aromatic depth. Its berries can be used fresh or dried to infuse spirits, while the branches are used for decoration, flavoring, or smoking cocktails.

FOREST SERENITY

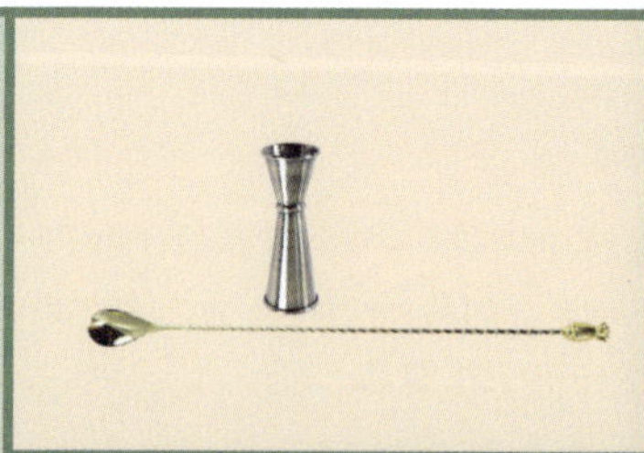

EQUIPMENT

GLASS TYPE: COGNAC

INGREDIENTS:

- 1⅓ fl oz (40 ml) gin Z44 (Roner)
- ⅔ fl oz (20 ml) pine liqueur (Quaglia)
- ⅔ fl oz (20 ml) lemon juice
- ⅓ fl oz (10 ml) pine syrup
- A few pine needles and buds
- BEER: Sour beer brewed with pine buds and needles
- Dried lime slice
- Ice

BUILD IN THE GLASS

1 – Make a pine syrup with needles and buds, reserving a sprig for garnish.
2 – Add all the ingredients except the beer and garnishes to the glass, fill with ice and stir.
3 – Top with beer, stir.
4 – Garnish: a sprig of fir and a slice of dried lime.

Sweet treats

This category conjures up rich, sweet, and indulgent notes, reminiscent of irresistible desserts and cozy treats. Gourmet touches such as cookies, chocolates, and nougat slivers add a soft, warm dimension to cocktail tasting, transforming the experience into an indulgent moment.

CHOCOLATE CHIPS

These cocoa treats enhance a range of cocktails, bringing a rich, indulgent, and luxurious note. They bring an element of refinement, and their ability to combine sweetness with robustness makes them invaluable mixology elements. Their aromatic richness and ability to balance flavors make them versatile ingredients.

CARAMEL

Whether liquid or solid, caramel is seductively versatile, adding indulgence and deep sweetness. With its smooth richness and deep aromas, it balances flavors without being overpowering, pairing well with a variety of spirits and other flavors. Its role goes beyond simple decoration, revealing depth and complexity that enrich the cocktail experience.

NOUGAT

The fragrant, honeyed, sweet notes, and sometimes the soft or crunchy aspect of nougat enrich cocktails, offering a delicious gourmet touch. Its sweet profile can complement comforting drinks, adding a mellow, pleasant dimension.

MARSHMALLOWS

These sweet treats soften more robust flavors, extending cozy fireside moments to cocktails, adding a gourmet touch and a unique sensory experience. Marshmallows offer a soft texture and generous flavor, enriching the taste palette of cocktails.

CANDIED FRUIT

These fruits, often macerated in sugar syrup, add a soft, sometimes crunchy texture to cocktails. Their bright visual presence adds a pleasing aesthetic to beverages, while contributing to their sweet taste profile. They can also be used to infuse spirits, enriching the aromatic base of cocktails.

OLD FASHIONED COZY RETREAT

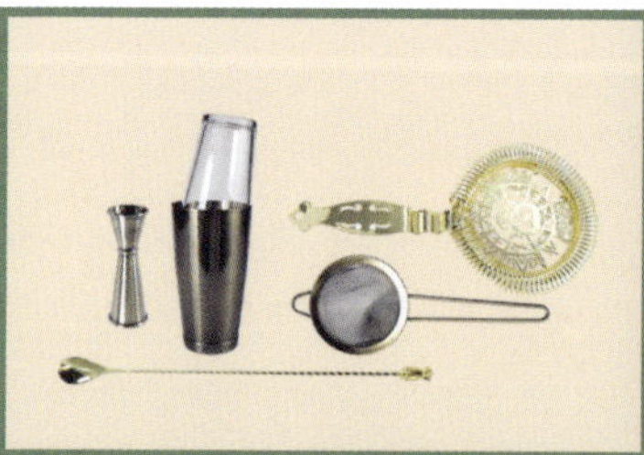

EQUIPMENT

GLASS TYPE: OLD FASHIONED

INGREDIENTS:

- 1⅓ fl oz (40 ml) Rammstein whisky
- ⅔ fl oz (20 ml) Cynar
- ⅓ fl oz (10 ml) chocolate syrup (Monin)
- BEER: Rye IPA
- A few toasted marshmallows (optional)
- 1 ice cube

IN THE SHAKER

1 –Toast the marshmallows and marinate in whisky for two days (optional).

2 – Add all ingredients except beer and marshmallows to shaker, fill with ice and shake.

3 – Serve over a cube of ice, filtering twice.

4 – Top with beer and stir.

5 – Garnish: a few toasted marshmallows.

Powdered

Often associated with baking, powders add sophistication and creativity to cocktails, combining distinct flavors and delicate textures to create a multisensory experience for the eyes and taste buds. Beyond their decorative aspect, they impart subtle aromatic notes, adding an intriguing dimension to cocktails.

CACAO

Cocoa powder, famous for its chocolatey character, enriches cocktails by adding a comforting and indulgent dimension. Its roasted aroma pairs well with a variety of drinks, offering subtle bitterness and additional aromatic richness. Sprinkled on the surface of cocktails or infused into mixes, it adds a desirable visual touch and delicious chocolate notes, especially in dark coffee, cream, and spirit-based drinks.

MATCHA TEA

With its emerald green hue and subtle bitterness, matcha balances sweet cocktails. Originally from Japan, it adds an herbaceous elegance and antioxidant benefits and is often used as a sprinkling for an attractive presentation.

COCONUT

With its exotic sweetness, coconut goes very well with fruit cocktails or sweet spirits. Its delicate aroma and fine texture make it easy to incorporate into drinks. Often used to decorate the rims of glasses, it can also be added directly to mixtures for a tropical touch.

MATCHA MARGARITA SOUR

EQUIPMENT

GLASS TYPE: MARGARITA

INGREDIENTS:

- 1⅓ fl oz (40 ml) tequila no. 1 Uno Blanco (123 Organic Tequila)
- ⅓ fl oz (10 ml) Cointreau
- ½ fl oz (15 ml) licorice syrup (Bacanha)
- ½ fl oz (15 ml) lime juice
- BEER: Rosemary Sour or any sour style beer
- ½ tsp matcha green tea blend
- Rosemary salt
- Crushed ice
- 1 slice of lime
- 1 sprig rosemary

IN THE SHAKER

1 – Rim glass with lime and rosemary salt.

2 – Add all ingredients except beer and garnishes to shaker, fill with ice and shake.

3 – Serve over crushed ice, filtering twice.

4 – Top with beer, stir.

5 – Garnish: a slice of lime and a sprig of rosemary.

Floral

Floral notes have become essential elements, offering a unique sensory experience. Their inventive use allows you to explore a variety of aromatic, visual, and taste profiles, adding a subtle, springtime touch to cocktails.

GUINEA SORREL

With its intense red petals, Guinea sorrel evokes the tropics and is often paired with vodka or gin. Its fruity, slightly tart tones offer versatility in cocktails. In addition to its visual appeal, its tartness harmoniously balances drinks, transforming them into exotic, refreshing creations.

POPPY

Poppies evoke sunny meadows with their delicate petals and bright red hues, adding a rustic touch. Infused to create syrups or floral waters, they add a sweet note to drinks. Its slightly sweet petals can be used as a garnish.

SWEET VIOLET

Delicate and fragrant, violets add beautiful purple color to drinks. Its fragrant essence is used to flavor syrups, vodka, or liqueurs, adding a fragrant, colorful nuance.

SAFFRON

Its precious pistils give a golden color, adding a touch of elegance and refinement. Its captivating fragrance and slightly bitter taste make saffron a precious ingredient for cocktails. Used as an infusion in a syrup, added in strands or powdered over the drink, it enhances aromatic profiles, offering subtle warmth, a floral touch, and an earthy nuance.

CANDY RED ROMANCE

EQUIPMENT

GLASS TYPE: FLUTE

INGREDIENTS:

- 1 fl oz of a lively, spicy, herbal gin
- ⅔ fl oz (20 ml) poppy liqueur
- ⅓ fl oz (10 ml) hibiscus syrup (Monin)
- A few strawberries (or 1⅓ fl oz [40 ml] juice)
- BEER: hibiscus wheat beer (white beer)
- 1 poppy
- Poppy candies
- Ice

IN THE SHAKER

1 – Crush poppy candies and rim one side of the glass with syrup and crushed candy.

2 – In the shaker, crush a few strawberries, add all ingredients except beer and poppy, fill with ice and shake.

3 – Serve through a double strainer.

4 – Top with beer, stir.

5 – Garnish: poppy candy rimming and a poppy.

Roasted

Toasty flavors bring depth and complexity to cocktails. Roasting releases deep aromas and rich, often bitter flavors that enhance beverages. These roasted notes add a new taste perspective, awakening the senses with warm, enveloping nuances.

COFFEE

Coffee, with its unique blend of roasted bitterness and sweetness, adds beautiful depth to cocktails. Used in a variety of forms, from whole beans to espresso, it transforms ordinary drinks into memorable experiences. From classics to more summery creations, everyone enjoys its stimulating touch. Roasted beans can also be used as a garnish for a crunchy bitterness. In short, coffee is a versatile and essential ingredient to awaken the senses.

ROASTED HAZELNUTS

Their rich, enticing tones make roasted hazelnuts an ideal garnish for adding warmth and complexity to cocktails. Roasting releases burnt notes that are perfect with spirits such as bourbon or cognac. Their subtle sweetness balances the flavors. Crushed on top of a cocktail or used to rim the glass, they offer an elegant presentation and a crunchy texture. Roasted hazelnut syrup provides a delicate infusion in the blend, and hazelnuts are also perfect for dessert cocktails.

ALMOND PRALINES

Delicate and crunchy, almond pralines make an exquisite topping. Their subtle combination of sweetness and crunchiness offers a refined taste experience, creating a perfect harmony. Their delicacy makes them a versatile garnish, ideal for enhancing or balancing the complexity of cocktails. When crushed to rim the glass, they add a captivating visual touch and a crunchy texture to every sip. Almond praline-based syrups offer a deliciously infused option for cocktails.

VELVET COFFEE

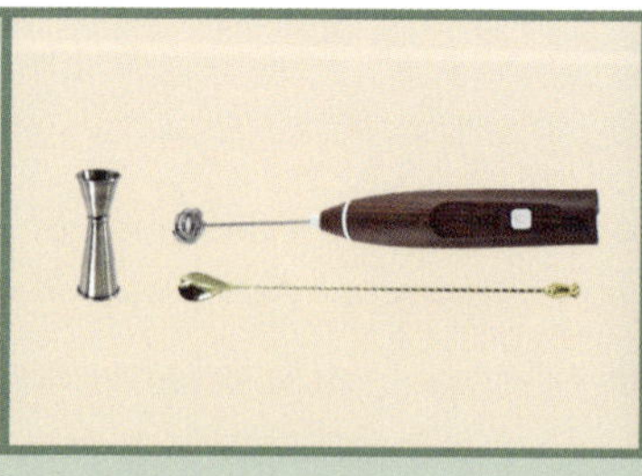

EQUIPMENT

GLASS TYPE: TASTING

DID YOU KNOW? Cold brew is the new black. To prepare cold brew, mix 80 g of coarsely ground coffee with one liter of water in a carafe. Leave to rest in the refrigerator for eighteen hours, then filter. You can adjust the concentration by adding water to suit your taste. This beverage can be used as a base for your cocktails.

INGREDIENTS:

- 1 espresso
- 1⅓ fl oz (40 ml) stout whisky (Black Irish)
- ⅔ fl oz (20 ml) chocolate cookie syrup (Monin)
- BEER: Imperial Stout (Jukebox Brewery)
- 1 cookie

BUILD IN THE GLASS

1 - Crumble the cookie and rim one side of the glass with chocolate syrup and cookie crumbs.
2 - Pour all ingredients except beer into the glass.
3 - Stir with a milk frother until you get a nice foam.
4 - Top with beer and stir.
5 - Garnish: cookie rimming.

Vegetables

Since you're supposed to eat five fruits and vegetables a day, why not cheat by adding some greens to your cocktails?

Vegetables add a refreshing touch, giving each drink a unique aspect. The combination of mixology with the freshness and diversity of vegetables offers crisp, juicy, earthy, or slightly bitter tones, enhancing the balance of each cocktail.

TOMATO

Tomatoes add a bold, refreshing aspect, broadening the aromatic palette of cocktails. Their versatility offers a tangy, earthy, and juicy touch, in the form of fresh juice, purée, or even dried. Their possibilities are vast, from light summer cocktails to complex, spicy creations. An essential vegetable garnish, tomatoes stimulate the senses and add a modern touch to cocktails.

BEETROOT

Often overlooked in mixology, beetroot nevertheless inspires unique cocktails. Its purplish hue and sweet, earthy profile offer a fascinating visual and taste experience. A versatile ingredient, it can be used in juices, syrups, or garnishes to add an innovative touch, particularly in light spirits. An intriguing option for exploring new sensory horizons.

BLACK GARLIC

Black garlic, a fermented version of fresh garlic, offers complex depth and intriguing sweetness to cocktails with notes of balsamic, caramel, and molasses. Used in syrup, paste, or infused in spirits, it adds an umami-rich gastronomic touch.

SOUTHERN VEGETABLE GARDEN

EQUIPMENT

GLASS TYPE: FANCY

INGREDIENTS

- 1⅓ fl oz (40 ml) tomato gin (Moletto)
- ⅓ fl oz (10 ml) lemon juice
- Yellow tomatoes (or 4 fl oz [120 ml] of juice)
- A few basil leaves
- 1 pinch of salt
- Ice
- 1 nasturtium leaf

BUILD IN THE GLASS

1 – Blend the yellow tomatoes.
2 – Squeeze and chop basil leaves finely then add to glass.
3 – Add the remaining ingredients, except beer and garnish, and stir.
4 – Add ice, top with beer and stir.
5 – Garnish: a nasturtium leaf.

Sour & savory

These dynamic ingredients, often used in cooking, offer stimulating notes of acidity that sometimes balance or spice up cocktails, adding a variety of notes ranging from sour to sweet.

BEER VINEGAR

Made from beer as its name suggests, beer vinegar is an innovation in the world of mixology, offering a range of complex, rich, acidic flavors. In smaller doses, it broadens the taste horizons, balancing profiles with deep acidity. Its versatile use allows you to explore new flavor facets, offering an interesting alternative to citrus fruits for a refined acidity. Used in syrup, it adds a tangy touch to glass rimming, enriching the tasting experience.

BALSAMIC CREAM

This delicate and velvety nectar of Italian gastronomy brings unexpected sophistication to modern cocktails, offering a distinct sweetness and remarkable aromatic complexity that elegantly enhances compositions. The velvety texture of balsamic cream and its sweet note add a balancing structure to drinks.

PICKLES

Often associated with appetizer platters, pickles are now finding their way into the world of cocktails, adding their crunch and tangy flavor to bold creations. Made from lacto-fermented brine, this tiny vinegary condiment adds an unexpected dimension to drinks, pushing the boundaries of innovation. Its crisp acidity and crunchy texture can balance flavor profiles, offering a unique sensory experience. Sliced and placed on the rim of the glass or added in juice, pickles offer a touch of spiciness and freshness, ready to awaken the taste buds with a unique flavor.

SMOKED OLD FASHIONED PICKLE SWEET & SOUR

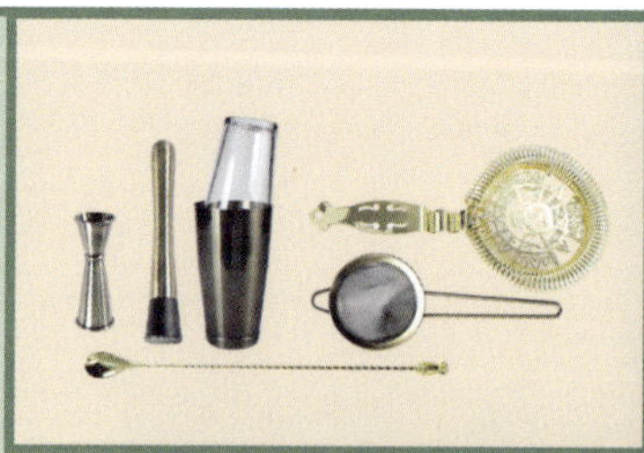

EQUIPMENT

GLASS TYPE: OLD FASHIONED

INGREDIENTS:

- 1⅓ fl oz (40 ml) pickle gin (Citadelle)
- ⅔ fl oz (20 ml) beer vinegar or white vinegar
- ⅔ fl oz (20 ml) pickle brine
- BEER: Märzen Rauchbier (Schlenkerla Brewery)
- 1 pickle, plus extra for garnish
- 1 ice cube

IN THE SHAKER

1 – Crush the pickle then add all ingredients except beer.
2 – Fill shaker with ice and shake.
3 – Serve over ice, double filtered.
4 – Top with beer, stir.
5 – Garnish: fanned pickle.

The diversity of cocktail garnishes offers endless possibilities. Each category adds its own touch, creating a captivating symphony of flavors. Garnishes add unique dimensions, expanding creative possibilities. By skillfully combining these elements, cocktails become true works of gustatory art, inviting drinkers on an exclusive sensory journey. Whether to stimulate the taste buds or to dazzle the eyes, the art of garnishing goes beyond mere decoration to become an essential part of the cocktail experience.

Ice

More than just an ingredient, ice is essential to the overall cocktail experience, controlling temperature, dilution, and texture according to preference.

TEMPERATURE

Ice cools the cocktail, which is essential for most drinks. A cocktail served cold is often more refreshing and enjoyable.

BINDING INGREDIENTS

When ice is shaken or stirred with the ingredients, it helps to seamlessly blend the different components of the cocktail.

ICE CUBE SIZES

Large: cube-shaped or spherical, they melt slowly and are perfect for drinks that should not be diluted too quickly.
Standard: versatile, good for most cocktails.
Crushed ice: cools quickly, perfect for juleps and Tiki drinks.
Long: ideal for drinks served in tall glasses.

INFLUENCE ON TASTE

Melting ice dilutes cocktails, softens strong drinks, and harmonizes flavors for a more enjoyable taste experience. Cooling also affects flavor perception – at lower temperatures, certain nuances may be less pronounced, while bitterness and alcohol may be reduced. What's more, ice can alter the texture of the cocktail – crushed ice creates a thicker, colder texture, while large cubes retain a smoother, less diluted texture.

DILUTION

Melting the ice is crucial as it dilutes the cocktail, balancing the flavors and mellowing strong alcohol.

THERMAL SHOCK – WHY ICE CRACKS

Ice cracks when it comes into contact with a warmer liquid due to the temperature difference. Avoid using ice immediately after taking it out of the freezer, as it is too cold and may crack or not dilute properly.

REDUCED ALCOHOL CONTENT

Dilution reduces the alcoholic strength of the cocktail, making the drink sweeter and easier to enjoy.

HEAT EXCHANGE

Ice absorbs the heat of the cocktail, causing it to melt and cool the drink while diluting it slightly. Smaller ice cubes, such as crushed ice, cool the cocktail faster due to their large surface area.

OIL CRYSTALLIZATION

Adding ice to some aniseed-flavored spirits can cause essential oils to crystallize, altering the drink's appearance and texture.

CLEANLINESS

Sometimes floating residues can be seen in certain aniseed-flavored alcoholic beverages, which can make you not want to finish your drink. This may be due to:

Impurities in the water: water containing impurities or dissolved minerals can cause residues to form in ice cubes after freezing.

Limescale: present in water, it can settle on ice cubes during production, especially in areas with hard water.

Deposits in the freezer: if the freezer is not regularly cleaned, deposits, dirt, and other particles can contaminate the ice cubes.

Residues in the container: if the container used to make the ice cubes is not clean, residues may be left in the ice cubes during freezing.

USE OF FILTERED WATER

Filtered water produces clearer ice cubes, without suspended particles, unwanted tastes or odors, which can improve cocktail quality.

USING ICE

Silicone molds: use silicone molds to obtain specific ice cube shapes and make them easier to remove.

Ice storage: keep ice in a clean, dry place to avoid flavor contamination.

HOW DO YOU MAKE CRUSHED ICE AT HOME?

A must-have for certain cocktails, so how can you make it without too much hassle?

There are two methods:

1 - To crush ice the old-fashioned way, use a tea towel: either hit the ice cubes wrapped in the tea towel with a rolling pin, or fold the corners of the tea towel and hit it against a sturdy surface to break the ice.

2 - A more modern option that requires an investment: use a manual or electric ice crusher to quickly and easily obtain evenly crushed ice.

COCKTAIL CATEGORIES

Classifying different cocktails into categories is essential to help understand the ingredients, preparation methods, and serving techniques.

Categories

SHOOTER

Appreciated for their fast-acting effect, shooters are often strong and concentrated, served in doses of 30 to 60 ml. Their small size makes them ideal for quick consumption, offering a short but intense tasting experience.

SHORT DRINKS

Cocktails in this category are often alcoholic, dry and powerful, with concentrated proportions of alcohol, often between 2⅓ fl oz (70 ml) and 4 fl oz (120 ml), with exceptions such as the Old Fashioned. They are served in small glasses, offering an intense experience in just a few sips, highlighting the quality of the ingredients. These drinks are appreciated for their simplicity and rapid effect, ideal for concise, memorable tasting.

LONG DRINKS

Less alcoholic, served in tall, slender glasses, they can be enjoyed over a longer period of time. In generous proportions, often over 4 fl oz (120 ml), they are diluted with ice cubes, fruit juices, or sodas to create refreshing, thirst-quenching drinks for prolonged enjoyment.

Types

BEFORE DINNER

Morning drinks, perfect for aperitifs, light, thirst-quenching, and often low in alcohol. They stimulate the appetite before meals and can be enjoyed in the afternoon on hot days.

AFTER DINNER

Along with liqueurs and spirits, they are often enjoyed late in the evening, after a meal, to relax and aid digestion. They can sometimes be more powerful, for lively evenings or special celebrations.

ALL DAY OR FANCY COCKTAILS

Often lighter, refreshing and original, designed to be enjoyed at any time of day, without necessarily stimulating the appetite or aiding digestion. They offer a refined tasting experience, perfect for special occasions, elegant brunches, or hot days. With a multitude of possible variations, experimentation with quality ingredients can result in truly unique creations.

These categories can overlap, and personal preferences are crucial to choosing the perfect cocktail at any time of day. This wide variety of cocktails means they can be enjoyed on any occasion.

HOT DRINKS

Perfect for chilly winter evenings, the hot cocktail is ideal for warming up indoors by the fire. These comforting drinks are enjoyed on occasions such as the festive season, or even, more simply, to cure a cold.

Each type of cocktail has its own distinctive characteristics, offering a variety of options to satisfy different tastes and preferences.

Families

By classifying cocktails according to their basic ingredients, it's easier to adapt recipes by varying the main spirit or chosen complements.

BUCK

Long drink served over ice in a long glass, combining brandies, citrus juices, ginger beer, or ginger ale. Refreshing and customizable, it's easy to prepare and appreciated for its thirst-quenching properties.

COBBLER

A long summer drink combining sherry, champagne, port, and vermouth with brandies such as cognac and whisky. Served over crushed ice and mixed with sugar and sparkling water, it is often accompanied by a dash of lemon juice. Refreshing and flexible in the choice of ingredients, it's perfect for hot weather.

COLADA

A summery long drink that evokes vacations and relaxing moments by the sea. Prepared in a blender or shaker with coconut cream, tropical fruit juice, and rum, it offers a creamy, exotic profile, perfect for summer refreshment.

COLLINS

Served straight on ice in tall glasses, this long drink offers thirst-quenching refreshment. It combines spirits, lemon juice, sugar syrup, and sparkling water, with a garnish of cherry brandy and a slice of lemon.

COOLER

This long drink, derived from the Fizz or Collins, offers a refreshing low-alcohol experience. It's made with brandy, sugar, fruit juice and topped up with a carbonated drink such as water, cider, champagne, or soda. Served over ice, it is often garnished with citrus peel.

CRUSTA

This short drink, similar to a sour, features a sugar rimming and a large citrus peel. Served over ice in a tasting glass, it combines brandy, lemon, sugar, concentrated bitter or liqueur for an elegant, fragrant drink.

CUP

This often-festive communal drink includes punches such as sangria. Served in a cup or bowl, it mixes spirits, fruit, spices, fruit juices, or sodas.

DAISY

Short drink, derived from a sour, incorporating aromatic liqueurs and syrup to replace sugar. It often includes a base spirit, lemon juice, sometimes curaçao and sparkling water, with the addition of liqueurs such as Cointreau or Grand Marnier for an extra aromatic dimension.

EGG NOG

A traditional Christmas long drink served hot or cold. It often contains milk, cream, eggs, sugar, and spices such as cinnamon or nutmeg. It is often flavored with rum, brandy, or bourbon.

FIZZ

Long drink served with carbonated drinks or sodas, creating a light, effervescent blend. Often served without ice and garnished with a slice of lemon, it can include a variety of spirits.

FLIP

This creamy cocktail, served hot or cold, is made in a shaker with fortified wine or brandy, egg yolk, sugar, and eau-de-vie. Often sprinkled with nutmeg, this short drink contains no cream or milk, unlike eggnog.

FLOATER

Often made with ice-cold sparkling water and an additional ingredient such as liqueurs or dense syrups, poured gently over the back of a spoon to float on top. It adds a unique visual dimension, intensifying taste and adding an appealing aesthetic. You can experiment with different colors to make a visual impression. It's important to choose liquids that don't mix immediately, creating a distinct separation between the layers.

FRAPPÉ

Short drink shaken, strained, and served over crushed ice with a short straw. An eau-de-vie or liqueur frappé poured directly over crushed ice without prior mixing, ideally from a chilled bottle. The spirit or liqueur can also be mixed with crushed ice and poured unfiltered into a glass.

FROZEN

A frosty short drink made in a blender with crushed ice, giving a slushy texture. Traditionally served with a straw, it is best enjoyed slowly. Often called "frozen" or "blended drink," it is enjoyed for its freshness and smooth consistency.

GROG (HOT TODDY)

Usually made with various ingredients such as rum or whisky, lemon juice, hot water or hot tea, sugar or honey, and sometimes spices such as cinnamon. Always served hot, it is comforting in cold weather and often considered a traditional remedy for sore throats, colds, or simply to warm up. Its many variations allow it to be adapted to personal preferences.

HIGHBALL

Easy to make, served over ice in a tumbler, this popular, refreshing long drink combines eau-de-vie with soda or tonic.

JULEP

Considered a sub-category of smashes, this thirst-quenching cocktail highlights the freshness of crushed mint. Prepared with bourbon, rye whisky or cognac, sugar, crushed ice, and mint leaves, it is served in hammered metal containers. Offering a soothing, summery touch, it embodies casual elegance.

MULE

Characterized by the use of ginger beer, it is often served in a copper glass with eau-de-vie, lemon juice and sometimes syrup. It is known for its freshness, simplicity, and distinct association with ginger.

OLD FASHIONED

A simple, elegant short drink that highlights the quality of the ingredients. Made directly in a glass of the same name, it is composed of sugar soaked in bitters, water (ice cubes), and eau-de-vie. Often served over ice with a slice of orange or lemon and a cherry eau-de-vie, it highlights the pure essence of the spirit, offering a robust and timeless tasting experience.

RAINBOW LAYERS

Layered and composed of ingredients such as colored liqueurs, fruit juices, and syrups, this cocktail is often served in a narrow shooter-style glass to preserve the separation of the layers.

PLANTER'S PUNCH

Refreshing and ideal for gatherings, this cocktail is often prepared in large quantities in a bowl. Served in large containers, it is exotic and intended for several guests. Made from a variety of ingredients – fruit juices, spirits (often rum), sodas, and sometimes fruit pieces – it's easy to make in large quantities, making it popular at events.

RICKEY

Lightly sweetened, this long drink Collins adaptation is made with spirits, lime juice, sparkling water or soda and ice. With no added sugar, it is appreciated for its simplicity and freshness.

SANGAREE

Originally from the British West Indies, it is made with beer, port, wine, or sherry, instead of eau-de-vie, and garnished with grated nutmeg.

SLING

Often served over ice in long glasses, this family takes its name from the famous "Singapore sling." Renowned for its freshness and balance between alcohol and fruity flavors, it uses brandy, tart fruit juice, sugar, sparkling water, and sometimes bitter ingredients.

SMASH

Similar to juleps, this cocktail is associated with warm weather. It uses fresh fruit such as oranges, mint, sugar or syrup, and a base spirit, usually bourbon. Prepared by gently crushing the fresh mint to release its fragrance, it is then served over crushed ice. Smashes share some characteristics with juleps, but the main difference is in the flexibility of the ingredients. Smashes can use different fruits, herbs, and spirits to create a variety of flavors, while juleps are more traditional. So, all juleps are smashes, but not all smashes are juleps.

SNAPPER

Appreciated for its invigorating character and brunch drink qualities, this family varies on the Bloody Mary theme with key differences in ingredients. The best-known is the gin snapper, or red snapper, which replaces vodka with gin, offering a more aromatic, herbaceous touch. Like Bloody Mary, snappers contain tomato juice, lemon juice, Worcestershire sauce, hot sauce, and other seasonings, but the choice of main spirit gives them their distinctive character.

SOFT DRINK

Also known as a "mocktail" or "virgin," it offers an alternative to traditional non-alcoholic cocktails. Served hot or cold, they're often made with fresh ingredients, syrups, and aromatic garnishes to ensure an experience as enjoyable as alcoholic cocktails. Ideal for those who prefer to avoid alcohol or want a new experience, they are suitable for all occasions: designated drivers, people with health concerns, or those looking for creative alternatives.

SOUR

Short drink made in a shaker, combining eau-de-vie, lemon or lime, sugar and a brandy-soaked cherry. The tart taste of lemon balances the strength of the alcohol, creating a refreshingly harmonious drink. This is the basis of many other families.

SPARKLING

Often served in a flute or coupe and associated with festive occasions, this sparkling, refreshing cocktail uses ingredients such as champagne, sparkling wine, cider or beer, adding a pleasant effervescence.

TIKI

Served in decorative glasses and often accompanied by crushed ice, this cocktail is characterized by the use of rum, tropical ingredients like coconut water or exotic juices, sweet syrups, and sometimes spices like cinnamon and nutmeg. Decorated with extravagant garnishes, it is strongly influenced by Polynesian and Hawaiian culture.

THE BASICS OF COCKTAIL CREATION

Let's demystify cocktail making.

You don't have to be a mixology expert to make good cocktails.

Just like in the kitchen, it's possible to enjoy cooking without being a chef.

Here are a few tips to help you create successful cocktails and impress your friends every time.

RULES TO FOLLOW

They are simple but crucial:

- **Follow hygiene standards:** wash your hands, maintain strict hygiene, and make sure the glass is clean.
- **No more than seven liquid or solid ingredients:** for a harmonious balance, limit yourself to seven ingredients. This maintains aromatic complexity without confusing the palate.
- **Respect the balance (very important):** the balance between taste and alcohol is crucial. Each ingredient must play its part without dominating, ensuring a consistent and enjoyable taste experience.
- **Measure accurately:** the success of a cocktail depends on the proportions, so always measure your liquids. Use a jigger to ensure good measurements. As in cooking,

precision is essential. Although bartenders pour with ease, this skill takes years of practice. Too much or too little of an ingredient can alter the result.

- **Don't mix randomly:** each ingredient has its role to play, so avoid random combinations. Choose complementary elements to create a symphony of flavors and aromas rather than an indistinct chaos.
- **Use edible garnishes as much as possible:** keep decorations simple. Avoid excessive decorations such as palm tree and umbrella-shaped picks. Find inspiration from cocktail bars or videos on social media – greenery, edible flowers, peels, glaze, fruit wedges, or sometimes, simply nothing.
- **Details matter:** every detail counts. Choose the right glass, pay attention to decoration, create the right atmosphere, and use high-quality ice to control the dilution and temperature of the cocktail. Tasting begins with the eyes.
- **No more plastic straws:** using reusable metal or bamboo straws enriches the tasting experience. These environmentally friendly alternatives are now affordable and readily available.
- **Keep it cool:** don't skimp on the ice. Too little ice dilutes the cocktail and makes it less refreshing. Be generous, fill the shaker with ice for optimal freshness and a better taste experience.
- **Chill your glass before serving:** for cocktails without ice, a lukewarm glass increases the temperature of the cocktail. There are two solutions: add ice cubes with water and remove them before serving or place the glass in the freezer for 10 to 15 minutes. This adds a nice, frosted touch to the presentation.
- **Choose the right temperature:** this is crucial for optimizing flavors. Stirring a cocktail cools it effectively. Cold sparkling drinks retain their effervescence, lowering the temperature and slowing down the melting of the ice, which reduces dilution. For dissolved gas to remain longer, the drink should be as cold as possible.
- **Add the ice last.**
- **Minimize dilution:** adding ice last prevents premature dilution if you are interrupted before finishing the cocktail. This ensures that the ingredients are not wasted, and that the taste and quality of the finished cocktail remain intact.

- **Temperature control:** adding ice at the very end, just before serving, allows precise control of temperature and dilution, ensuring that the cocktail is fresh and balanced when served.

BALANCE

Subtle harmony

A well-balanced cocktail is like a melody in which each flavor must find its place. The sugar is subtle, the acidity caressing rather than intrusive, the alcohol adds warmth, and the bitterness gently dissipates on the finish, offering a refined and pleasurable experience.

Culture and palate – a varied palette

The balance of a cocktail varies according to culture and tradition. Taste preferences differ from one country to another, offering a fascinating diversity of flavors. What is balanced here may be perceived differently elsewhere. Tasting is very personal, influenced by history and customs.

Balance and imbalance – everything can change

In a well-balanced cocktail, each ingredient blends harmoniously to create a pleasurable drink. An unbalanced cocktail, where one flavor dominates, can be surprising and often less enjoyable. Finding the right balance between sugar, acidity, alcohol, and bitterness is the essence of mixology. Aromatic balance is also crucial, as flavors blend together to create a memorable experience.

The secrets of balance

Balancing a cocktail requires skill and creativity. The choice of ingredients, precise proportions, and mixology techniques are essential to creating perfect harmony. The balance of a good cocktail lies in the precise measurement of each ingredient. Each flavor contributes without dominating, playing its part to create a harmonious experiences.

Rule of the 3 S's

A cocktail composed of at least two ingredients requires a balance between three key elements: sweet, sour, and strong, or the 3 S's.

Sweetness provides balance and smoothness. It can come from a variety of sources, such as sugar, liqueurs, creams, fruit, or syrups. Sour, often associated with citrus, certain flowers or vinegar elements, ensures cohesion. Strong, with the power of eaux-de-vie, creates the perfect harmony in the creation of a cocktail.

A word of advice: For beginners or those experimenting, pouring in the cheapest ingredients first makes sense to minimize waste, adjust flavors, and check quantities before adding expensive ingredients. There are two reasons for this:

- **Minimize waste:** if you make a mistake, it's cheaper to start again if the first ingredients are the cheapest. For example, making a mistake with lemon juice or simple syrup is less costly than with a premium spirit.
- **Stress-free learning:** beginners can practice and experiment without worrying about the high cost of mistakes. Mixology is both an art and a science, and reducing the cost-related stress encourages exploration and learning.

DISCOVERY AND CUSTOMIZATION

Creating a cocktail with your favorite beer means exploring its infinite nuances and possibilities.

Customize according to your preferences

Create your cocktail according to your mood, the occasion and the ingredients available. First, choose the base – alcoholic or non-alcoholic, hot or cold. Select a category of garnishes to guide you (pages 141 to 153). Choose a taste – sweet, salty, sour, bitter, umami, or rich. Next, choose a texture for your cocktail – it can be creamy, frothy, crunchy, smooth, light, etc. Decide whether you want a classic or surprising cocktail, gourmet, comforting, or energizing. Use ingredients that you like.

Explore different beer styles: every detail is intentional

Explore the vast diversity of beer styles to enrich your creations. From hoppy, bitter IPAs to roasty imperial stouts and tangy sours, each style offers unique characteristics that will influence your creations. Taste and understand their differences to refine your palate and discover your favorite profiles.

Choose beers, spirits, and ingredients to suit your taste. If you like fruity flavors, choose corresponding ingredients. Avoid smoky or peaty tones if you don't like them. Do you prefer caramelized, sweet notes? Try an aged rum or pastry bock beers with caramel.

Adventure and research

Exploring beer and spirits styles is an adventure. Step out of your comfort zone, discover new combinations, but above all choose a spirit that suits you.

MAKE A COCKTAIL WITH YOUR FAVORITE BEER

Describe beer's characteristics

Taste the beer before creating your cocktail to understand its characteristics. Identify scents: floral, fruity, spicy, earthy. Enjoy the tastes and aromas: malts, fruits, citrus, or others.

Evaluate the texture and body of your beer, from light to syrupy, to influence mouthfeel and structure. Pay attention to the bubbles – are they sparkling, prickly, lively, very effervescent, aggressive, or rather soft and subdued? This feature adds a dynamic dimension to your creation. Savor the finish – is it drying, slightly astringent, or does it leave a long-lasting mark? Do tastes and aromas last a long time? This final score will guide the choice of ingredients to complete the taste experience.

Identify the characteristics of eau-de-vie

To choose a spirit for cocktails, explore its sensory and structural characteristics, including terroir and geographic origin, which influence the aromatic profile. For example, Scotch whisky differs from American whisky. Identify dominant aromas (fruit, spices, herbs, etc.) and specific flavors. The alcohol content influences the strength of the cocktail and sensory perception in the mouth. Evaluate its texture – whether delicate or robust – and consider the finish. Choose a liqueur or an eau-de-vie that works well with your chosen beer. Make sure the flavor profiles blend harmoniously.

A few examples of pairings

Here are a few ideas of styles and eaux-de-vie that might go well together.

For light beers such as pilsners, international pale lagers, or pale ales, choose light spirits such as gin for its delicacy or vodka for its neutrality. Their subtle profiles won't overpower the delicate notes of these beers. Grain vodka accentuates the cocktail's power, while potato vodka allows the aromas of the other ingredients to shine through.

A triple sec adds a touch of citrus and sweetness, pairing well with the light, hoppy notes of these beers for a refreshing aroma profile.

For sweet, malty beers such as Irish red ales, Märzens, autumn beers, and amber Bière de Garde, opt for light whiskies with mild profiles such as bourbon or rye whisky. Their woody, vanilla, and honey notes complement the toasty and brioche aromas of these beers. A coffee liqueur adds roasted, slightly sweet notes that enhance the maltiness. A hazelnut liqueur offers tones of roasted hazelnuts that pair well with the grain and occasional light caramel found in amber ales.

To accompany lighter, darker, roasted, and toasted beers like stouts or porters, choose spirits with delicate profiles. Subtly peated Scotch whiskies highlight malt, fine peat, and vanilla; Irish whiskies, renowned for their smoothness, are also a good option. Gins with citrus or berry accents add aromatic complexity to dry stouts. For rums, opt for light amber options with notes of vanilla, caramel, and dried fruit to complement the malt nuances of porters. A chocolate liqueur or crème de cacao brings chocolatey nuances that pair perfectly with the roasted notes, while crème de menthe offers a minty freshness that contrasts nicely with the rich, toasted tones of these beers, making for an interesting combination, especially for fans of chocolate and minty flavors.

Strong pale beers such as Triples, strong Belgian blondes, or Hellesbocks, with their fruity, herbaceous, spicy, and malty esters, go well with brandy, adding sophistication to these beers. For example, the dried fruit, honey, and vanilla notes of cognac blend with their fruity and malty nuances. Calvados is an excellent option, especially with grain, brioche, citrus, and spicy beers, as its notes of ripe apple, vanilla, and wood complement their complex characteristics. The balance between the richness of calvados and the malty aromas of strong blonde beers offers a harmonious tasting experience.

To accompany more powerful, roasted, and complex beers like imperial stouts and Baltic porters, choose robust eaux-de-vie to enhance the taste experience. Peated whiskies, with their smoky, earthy notes, pair well with roasted malts, offering a rich, robust experience. Fruit eaux-de-vie such as plum, cherry, or pear add an extra dimension with their fruity traits. An artisanal coconut liqueur brings a tropical touch, complementing the cocoa profiles and adding exoticism. For a spicy note, a pepper liqueur goes well with their robust character.

For bitter, hoppy beers like IPAs, New Zealand pilsners, or American pale ales, choose floral or spicy spirits to complement the hop aromas. With its botanical notes, gin adds an herbaceous, summery complexity, while spiced rum offers a warmth that pairs well with the hops. The spiced rum's aromas of caramel, vanilla, and cinnamon add depth without being overpowering. Peach liqueur brings a fruity sweetness that balances the hop aromas, offering a subtle finesse. Melon or mango liqueur adds a tropical freshness that blends harmoniously with the fruity hop aromas.

Barleywines and old ales, with their malty, vinous strength and comforting, aged feel, pair well with robust eaux-de-vie for an enriched taste experience. Aged brandies such as Armagnac are a perfect match, accentuating their depth with complex notes of dried fruit, caramel, and wood, complementing the rich, aged profiles of these beers. A well-balanced bourbon can also add notes of vanilla, oak, and caramel that blend harmoniously with the malty, caramelized, and sometimes vinous nature of these strong beers.

Sour beers such as lambics, sours, straight sours, or fruited sours lend themselves well to exploring fruity spirits that enhance their sour flavor. A fruit brandy, with its rich notes of ripe fruit, adds a fruity dimension, while raspberry or cherry brandy intensifies the fruity nuances of Gueuzes. Pear schnapps offers a lightly sweet, refreshing experience, creating a harmony of acidity and fruity notes. A gin with citrus or berry notes can pair nicely with these beers, its floral tones complementing the acidic characteristics while adding an aromatic dimension. For more delicate sours like Berliner Weisse and Gose, gin or tequila are wise choices, bringing subtle notes that complement rather than dominate the delicate profiles of these beers.

Beers incorporating spices, vegetables, herbs, or specific aromatic ingredients, such as coriander, pepper, cardamom, cloves, ginger, cinnamon, orange peel, or gingerbread, are often seasonal, such as Christmas beers or pumpkin ales. To accompany these beers, spiced gins and herb-infused vodkas harmoniously complement the spicy characteristics.

Absinthe, an herbal drink, can also be an interesting option. Ginger liqueur adds a spicy warmth and a tangy note that complements the spicy characteristics of beers, creating an interesting synergy between the ginger notes and the spices present in the beer.

Dubbels are complex beers, characterized by rich sweet flavors, malty, caramelized, cooked, and dried fruit aromas. Oak-aged bourbon adds notes of vanilla, caramel, and wood that complement its malty tones, creating a harmonious tasting experience. Port, especially a ruby, brings fruity, spicy, and sweet notes that pair well with its malty profile and hints of dried fruit. For Quadrupels, which are more robust and complex, marked by smooth and malty flavors, a peaty whisky harmonizes with the malty tones and hints of dried fruit, adding smoky accents. Cognac brings notes of candied fruit, caramel, and vanilla that complement its sweet and malty characteristics.

To accompany light, refreshing Belgian wheat beers, which are often spicy and citrusy, a pear eau-de-vie adds a subtle fruity sweetness that pairs well with their lightness, accentuating the floral and citrus notes. A triple sec intensifies the citrus aromas already present, creating a lively, refreshing experience. For German beers with a malty, yeasty, phenolic profile with hints of banana and spices such as cloves or pepper, a wheat schnapps complements the malty side, while an amber rum adds a touch of vanilla and caramel for more depth.

Exploring banana or chocolate spirits with a Dunkelweizen is intriguing and offers interesting combinations. A banana liqueur enhances the banana notes already present, creating harmony with the beer, while a chocolate liqueur adds a sweet, chocolatey touch, complementing the beer's malty tones for a dessert dimension. American wheats with their malty, brioche, citrus, spicy, and floral notes go well with a subtly citrusy gin for a refreshing dimension, or a citrus liqueur to accentuate the floral tones, creating a vibrant experience.

Test and adjust

Once you have chosen your base, test and adjust the balance. For more acidity, add citrus juice; for more sweetness, adjust the sugar. Adapt the ingredients to your preference – sweet, fruity, rich, or dry.

Play with textures

Experiment with ingredients that enrich the cocktail's texture, such as egg white for a frothy texture, or specific syrups for a more syrupy feeling. Let your creativity run wild and draw inspiration from existing practices. Explore a variety of garnishes, fresh or dehydrated, which add not only a visual touch but also a new aroma.

Add unexpected ingredients

Feel free to experiment with less conventional ingredients, such as homemade infusions or syrups, or unusual spices for a personal touch.

Trust your palate

Trust your palate, adjusting the proportions until the cocktail fully reflects your preferences. Each ingredient is essential to the alchemy of your cocktail, so understand their characteristics to create harmony. Let your favorite beer guide you and explore the infinite creativity it can inspire. Visit your local wine shops or breweries, try new styles, and choose the beer that will spark your passion for creating unique and personalized cocktails.

Adapt to seasons and the occasion

Some styles of beer are better suited to certain seasons or occasions, just like certain cocktails. Adapt your choices to the context, your mood, and the special moments you want to celebrate. Of course, you can enjoy any type of beer or cocktail at any time – it's all a matter of choice. When it comes to fruit, I recommend adapting your cocktails to the seasons for ethical reasons. For example, using frozen or puréed fruit can be a responsible alternative if fresh fruit is not in season.

REINVENTING A CLASSIC COCKTAIL WITH BEER

Reinventing an existing cocktail with a beer you love is a creative adventure that can bring a new, fun dimension to a classic drink. Here's how it works, in just a few steps.

Choose your cocktail

Select a cocktail that inspires you and that you'd like to reinvent.

Understand its nature

Break down the ingredients, flavors, aromas, and smells of the original cocktail to understand how the beer could blend in harmoniously.

Choose the right beer

Depending on the base cocktail, choose a beer to complement and enhance it. Identify the affinities and synergies between the beer and the spirits. If necessary, change the beer.

Adapt the ingredients

Think about the ingredients in the base cocktail and adjust them to incorporate the beer. This may involve changing an ingredient or finding ingredients that go well with the chosen beer.

Make sure it's balanced

Make sure that the flavors of the beer and the other ingredients balance each other. The beer should not dominate, but rather complement the cocktail in a subtle way, and vice versa.

Experiment

Feel free to explore different proportions and combinations. Experiment to find the perfect balance that enhances the beer while respecting the essence of the base cocktail.

Pay attention to presentation

Presentation is crucial. Choose an appropriate, clean glass and garnish the cocktail with elements that reflect your vision. Visually, the reinvented cocktail should be captivating.

Take notes

Take notes on any adjustments you make throughout the process. This will help you perfect the recipe and understand how different styles of beer interact with different cocktails. By following these steps, you can reinvent a beer cocktail in a thoughtful, creative way. Exploring the nuances between beer styles and cocktails offers fertile ground for innovation.

Feel free to casually reinvent cocktails. Be daring and try bold combinations of beer, spirits, and other ingredients to create unique recipes. Whether your taste journey is punctuated by renowned classics or hidden gems, the unified worlds of mixology and beerology offer an infinite canvas where every sip is an experience in itself.

Starting with creating a cocktail with a beer you've enjoyed, or reinventing an existing cocktail with this beer will stimulate your creativity.

I'm sure you're beginning to see the fascinating art behind the alchemical combination of elements. You now understand the importance of knowing the various ingredients in your recipe, and how one style of beer can pair with a variety of spirits. With this approach, I encourage you to let your creativity run wild. The creative possibilities are endless, and I'm sure you're ready to embark on an exceptional taste adventure. Now, let's explore some techniques.

PREPARATION TECHNIQUES

MIXING INGREDIENTS

Shake in a shaker

When to use it? A shaker is essential for mixing various ingredients to obtain a creamy texture. To save time and prevent ice cubes from melting too quickly, prepare the equipment, ingredients, and garnish in advance, regardless of the type of shaker you use.

THE PARISIAN CONTINENTAL

1 – First option: add the ingredients, then the ice; second option: fill the large tumbler ⅔ full with ice to chill it.

2 – Add ingredients (two possibilities):

- Strain the melted water from the ice before adding the ingredients to the large tumbler. The first instinct is often to put the ice in first, then the ingredients, but if you forget something or are interrupted, the ice will melt and the cocktail will be ruined.
- Alternatively, pour the ingredients into the lid and strain the melted water from the large bowl. Here's a little trick to prevent excess melted water from diluting the ingredients: put the ice in the large tumbler and place the lid inside so you can add the ingredients. This will allow them to start cooling without coming into direct contact with the ice.

3 - Pour the contents of the lid into the tumbler and secure it tightly. Hold the shaker firmly on both sides and shake vigorously for about 15 seconds while holding it horizontally.
4 - Open and strain the mixture through a fine Hawthorne strainer.
5 - Add the garnish to decorate the cocktail.

THE COBBLER

1 - Fill the large tumbler ⅔ full with ice.
2 - Strain the melted ice before pouring in the ingredients, using the measuring cap if it is graduated. If not, use a jigger.
3 - Close the lid with the cap, hold the shaker on both sides and shake vigorously for about 15 seconds.
4 - Remove the cap and serve through the built-in strainer, which will hold back the ice and large pieces more than a fine strainer.
5 - To finish, add the garnish.

THE BOSTON

1 - Fill the large tumbler ⅔ full with ice.
2 - Fill the glass with the ingredients.
3 - Strain the melted ice.
4 - Empty the contents of the glass into the tumbler and fit it firmly into place at an angle. Make sure it is tightly sealed by tapping it firmly. This will create a vacuum and hold everything in place.
5 - Hold both parts firmly and shake vigorously for about 15 seconds.
6 - Give a sharp tap on the side to remove the glass by gently turning it. Serve in the glass using a fine Hawthorne strainer to retain any solids.
7 - Add the garnish.

TIP: Even though the glass cup is sturdy, it can break due to sudden changes in temperature. For beginners, we recommend using a stainless steel or plastic cup.

The dry shake

To achieve a smooth emulsion, cocktails containing eggs, milk, or cream are first shaken without ice, then shaken a second time with ice. Some use the Hawthorne strainer's spring to act as a whisk during the first shake, which creates a better emulsion thanks to the warmer temperature and the spring.

The difference between shaking and stirring

Stirring or shaking a cocktail cools and dilutes the ingredients. The shaker, which is more intense, creates air bubbles, giving the cocktail a cloudy and airy appearance. Although the rule is not always followed, clear drinks are often mixed, while those with cloudy ingredients such as fruit juice, milk, egg white, or cream are shaken.

Shake: shake ingredients vigorously with ice in a shaker to mix and chill them.

Dilute: add ice or water to a cocktail to reduce its alcohol content.

Stir

IN A MIXING GLASS

When to use it? For clear and delicate cocktails, especially those made primarily with spirits.

1 - Chill the cocktail glass with ice and water to make the sides of the glass cold. Once cold, empty the glass, then refill with ice.
2 - Add the various ingredients to the mixing glass.
3 - Use a mixing spoon to stir the ingredients for about 30 seconds.
4 - Strain the contents through a fine Hawthorne strainer and serve in the glass.
5 - Decorate the glass if desired.

THROWING/CUBAN ROLL

Transferring the liquid mixture from one container to another several times to aerate and mix the ingredients provides pronounced dilution and aeration, less aggressive than vigorous shaking in a shaker. It's a refined, visual technique for preparing elegantly mixed drinks.

BUILD IN THE GLASS

When to use it? For simple cocktails without a shaker or mixing glass.

1 - Place the ice cubes in the glass.
2 - Add each ingredient directly to the glass.
3 - Stir gently with a bar spoon.
4 - Serve as is.

ON THE ROCKS

When to use it? To serve a cocktail directly over ice.

1 - Place ice cubes in the glass.
2 - Pour the cocktail directly over the ice cubes.
3 - Stir gently if necessary.

TOP OFF

When to use it? At the end of the preparation phase, to adjust or dilute the alcohol content – usually by adding a soft drink, soda, or water.

1 - Choose a complementary liquid.
2 - Pour slowly into the cocktail.
3 - Mix gently with a bar spoon.
4 - Adjust to taste preferences.

Muddling

It's difficult to muddle fruit effectively in the shaker when all the liquid ingredients are present, as fruit tends to slip and float. This can result in uneven juice and flavor extraction. It's best to muddle the fresh fruit on its own, then add the remaining ingredients.

FILTRATION

Hawthorne strainer: shaker filtering (hawthorne strain)

When to use it? After shaking a cocktail.

Pour the mixture through the strainer with a Boston shaker, Continental shaker, or mixing glass over the glass.

Julep strainer: filter through the mixing glass

When to use it? After preparing a cocktail.

Pour the mixture through the strainer via a mixing glass or shaker over the glass.

DOUBLE FILTRATION (DOUBLE STRAIN-FINE STRAIN)

Why use it? For better filtration of fine particles.

Pour the mixture through a fine strainer in addition to the Hawthorne or Julep strainer.

In this book, double filtration is recommended for two main reasons. Firstly, it improves clarity and texture. By effectively removing small pieces and fine particles, it ensures a visually pure beverage with a smooth texture, for a more refined experience.

Second, double filtering ensures optimal dilution control. By removing tiny pieces of ice broken during shaking, it prevents excessive dilution of the cocktail after serving, thus maintaining its flavor profile for longer.

Consistent taste experience: with no annoying chunks, every sip is consistent with your expectations, enhancing your tasting experience.

Neat presentation: a double-filtered cocktail looks better, especially for clear drinks served in transparent glasses.

For more efficiency

To prevent residue from clogging the fine strainer during filtration, gently tapping the strainer with the shaker or the back of a spoon can help dislodge particles and allow the liquid to flow more easily.

- **Gentle use:** tap the strainer gently to prevent unwanted debris from passing into the cocktail. A light tap is all it takes.
- **Avoid tapping the rim of the glass:** tapping the strainer against the rim of the glass can chip it or cause unwanted fragments to fall into the cocktail.
- **Regular cleaning:** to avoid clogging the strainer when filtering several cocktails, rinse it under cold water between each use.

For effective filtration, especially with cocktails containing fine particles, take your time to ensure a flawless presentation and an optimal taste experience.

CLARIFICATION (MILK PUNCH)

Clarifying a cocktail removes suspended particles to produce a clear drink without altering its profile. This technique aims to clarify while preserving or enhancing aromas and flavors.

COAGULATION

Adding a coagulating agent, such as lemon juice in Milk Punch, causes proteins to coagulate. The acidity of the cocktail, often adjusted with a citrus fruit, causes the milk to curdle.

PARTICLE ATTRACTION

Coagulated proteins form clusters with suspended particles, gathering tannins, colorants, and other cloudy compounds into larger particles.

SEDIMENTATION AND FILTRATION

These larger particles are then easier to remove by sedimentation and filtration. Filtration, often using a coffee filter or fine cloth, retains the protein mass and suspended particles.

RESULTS

- **Clarity:** the drink becomes visually clearer, with improved transparency and brightness.
- **Texture:** clarification can also soften the texture of the drink, resulting in a smoother, more enjoyable mouthfeel.

FLAVOR PRESERVATION

Solid particles are removed, but volatile aromatic compounds are preserved or even concentrated, thereby enhancing the drink's flavor profile.

Clarifying a cocktail harmonizes flavors, provides a smooth texture, and visually transforms the drink.

Steps for clarifying a cocktail:

1 - **Cocktail preparation:** mix all cocktail ingredients containing an acidic element, such as lemon juice. Acidity is crucial for the clarification reaction.

2 - **Adding the milk:** pour the mixture into a container containing whole milk. It is important to pour the cocktail over the milk, and not the other way around, to promote uniform coagulation. The amount of milk required varies according to the acidity of the cocktail. Adjust according to your observations and experience.

3 - **Coagulation**: the acidity of the cocktail will curdle the milk. Let the mixture rest for 30 minutes to an hour. During this time, the coagulated proteins will capture the suspended particles and cloudy compounds.

4 - **Filtration:** after the resting period, the solids will separate from the liquid. Filter the mixture through a coffee filter placed in a strainer or fine sieve. This can take time, as the filter can become clogged with coagulated particles. Replace the filter if necessary to speed up the process.

5 - **Result:** the liquid obtained is clear, transparent and velvety, with no particles. Despite its clarity, the cocktail retains a rich complexity of flavors and a deep aromatic profile.

TIP: try this with different types of alcohol. The clarification technique works well with many cocktails.

GARNISHES

The art of mixology is not limited to flavors – aesthetics are crucial to the tasting experience. A visually captivating cocktail stimulates the senses, sparking anticipation and delight. This is why the visual aspect is essential in the art of cocktail making. A cocktail is defined by its flavor, aroma, and visual appeal. Vibrant color, intriguing texture, and elegant glassware are the first things that attract attention, making garnishes unnecessary. For simple cocktails, creative embellishments can add visual appeal. Meanwhile, glassware plays an important role, often accounting for over 50% of a cocktail's appeal by combining function and aesthetics.

GLASS RIMMING

Rimming the glass with powdered, crumbled, or flaked ingredients – the possibilities are endless. Make sure the rimming matches the cocktail. Rimming offers a variety of interesting advantages:

- **Aesthetics:** it adds an elegant, festive touch, making the cocktail more appealing, especially on special occasions.
- **Taste experience:** it can enhance the taste experience, for example, salt on a Margarita contrasts with the sweet and sour flavors, making them more pronounced. Sugar, on the other hand, softens and completes the flavors of a cocktail.
- **Mouthfeel:** the contrast between the cocktail's liquid and the ingredient's texture creates a unique sensory experience.
- **Tradition and recognition:** for certain classics, rimming is essential and contributes to their identity, such as the Crusta.

- **Only rim half the glass:** a good idea that gives you the choice to suit your preferences. You can experiment with the extra texture and flavor that rimming brings or enjoy the cocktail without this dimension.
- **Customization:** rimming the glass personalizes drinks. Choose between salt, sugar, or other ingredients depending on the cocktail. Here are a few great rimming ideas.

Sugar

Powdered sugar adds a touch of elegance. Brown sugar adds crunch and a hint of caramel, vanilla, or rum. Flavored and colored sugar adds colors and aroma.

Some ideas for original rimmings:

- **Cinnamon sugar:** evoking the festive season, it has a spicy aroma and goes well with cocktails based on chocolate, coffee, or orange liqueurs.
- **Brown sugar and orange zest:** for a summer evening or a tropical cocktail, it brings a caramelized sweetness. Orange zest, with its tangy sweetness and citrus aroma, is ideal for fruity or rum-based cocktails.
- **Sugar and black pepper:** for elegant evenings or refined cocktails, this unique blend offers crisp sweetness and a spicy tone. Perfect for whisky or gin-based cocktails, offering a bold contrast.
- **Sugar and chili powder:** for summer evenings or Mexican-themed parties, this blend gives sweetness and warmth, ideal for Margaritas or Bloody Marys, with a spicy touch that's not too strong.
- **Powdered sugar and dried edible flowers:** for wedding receptions or spring events, edible flowers add color and delicacy, creating an elegant and romantic rimming. Ideal for sweet, floral cocktails.

Salt

Salt can transform an ordinary cocktail into an extraordinary taste experience. By combining various salts with other ingredients, you can create unique rimming that enhance the flavor of beverages and add a fascinating visual and textural touch.

- **Fine sea salt and grapefruit zest:** perfect for summer cocktails, this blend adds a tangy freshness and a salty touch, ideal for Palomas or citrus cocktails.
- **Himalayan pink salt and powdered ginger:** perfect for exotic evenings, it adds a salty, warming and sweet note to cocktails.
- **Smoked salt and paprika:** for BBQs or evenings by the fire, adds a smoky tone and spicy sweetness, perfect for whisky or rustic cocktails.
- **Hawaiian black salt and black sesame seeds:** adds sophistication with its delicate, nutty aroma, ideal for modern, innovative cocktails.

Shavings and other ingredients

Rimming a glass goes beyond just sugar and salt – it can include shavings, ground or chopped ingredients that match the cocktail, adding a unique visual, textural, and flavorful aspect. Use candied lemon shavings for an intense lemony sweetness in gin or vodka-based cocktails. Chocolate brings a rich sweetness and melting texture, while coconut adds an exotic note with a slightly crunchy texture. Parmesan shavings add a salty, umami touch, ideal for tomato-based or Italian-inspired cocktails. To make them stick, use balsamic cream with its distinctive sweet-and-sour taste and thick consistency.

Powders are ideal for their ability to dissolve or blend harmoniously in liquids, adding flavor and color.

Take some sweet, rich, fragrant cocoa powder for gourmet cocktails made with chocolate, coffee, caramel, and vanilla. For rimming a glass, use a flavored syrup or chocolate liqueur. The slightly bitter matcha green powder is ideal for Japanese or healthy cocktails.

Chopped herbs such as basil, rosemary, thyme, and mint offer a vibrant freshness, ideal for cocktails with gin, vodka, or Mediterranean cuisine, while gingerbread or crumbled speculoos add a gourmet touch to winter cocktails.

Rimming the glass (the rim or drinking edge)

1 – Put the solid rimming ingredients in a shallow dish and the liquid rimming base in another, enough to cover the rim of the glass.

2 – Moisten the rim of the glass by rubbing it with a citrus fruit wedge or dipping it in the liquid rimming base.

3 - Dip the glass into the plate of solid rimming ingredients, turning it slightly to ensure an even rim.
4 - Gently shake the glass to remove any excess. Leave to rest for a few minutes to allow the rimming to adhere before pouring in the cocktail.
5 - Serve gently without touching the rim to keep the rimming intact.

Rimming the glass wall (the outside surface of the glass)

1 - Apply the syrup with a brush to the outside of the glass.
2 - Roll the glass in the rimming mixture placed on a plate - or sprinkle the mixture directly onto the glass.
3 - Tap to remove excess. For a detailed design, use a stencil.

FLAMBÉING

This impressive technique intensifies flavors and makes a show of itself when presented. More than just a way to heat up a cocktail, it adds an extra dimension to the tasting experience, perfect for impressing guests.

- **Choice of alcohol:** opt for strong spirits (over 40% ABV) for flambéing, as they ignite easily.
- **Safety first:** flambé in a well-ventilated area away from any flammable materials. Be ready to extinguish the flames if necessary.
- **Aromatic and flavor effects:** flambéing can alter the alcohol, imparting caramel or nutty notes, and it releases aromas that enrich the cocktail's olfactory experience.
- **Visual impact:** it's a great way to impress guests. The spectacle makes for a surprising show.
- **Practice and experimentation:** practice flambéing with small quantities of alcohol in a controlled environment to master this technique.

Flambéing technique:

- **Direct flambéing:** ignite a cocktail by pouring strong alcohol (at least 40% A.B.V.) over the top to create a caramelized top layer and add aroma.
- **Indirect flambéing:** gently heat the alcohol in a small saucepan until hot but not boiling, then ignite with a long lighter or match. Transfer the flaming alcohol to the glass using a saucepan with a pouring spout, tilting it gently to pour slowly and safely. Be sure to maintain a safe distance between the saucepan and the glass to prevent accidental spillage. The flame follows the liquid, creating a beautiful visual effect.
- **Flambéing an ingredient:** flambé an ingredient such as orange zest, a sugar cube, a marshmallow, or a cinnamon stick separately to release the essential oils and concentrated aromas, then add them to the cocktail.

ICE CUBE DECORATION

Decorate ice cubes for an original aesthetic touch in your cocktails.

Ice cubes with fresh fruit, spices, and herbs

Add berries, fruit slices, citrus peel, cinnamon stick, star anise, or herbs to ice cube trays before filling with water and freezing. They will be trapped in the ice, revealing their aromas as they melt.

Fruit juice ice cubes

Freeze fruit juice to obtain colorful ice cubes that add an extra aromatic touch to the cocktail as they melt.

Frozen edible flowers

Freeze edible flowers for a summery visual effect. Make sure the flowers are edible and pesticide-free.

Patterned ice cubes

Use uniquely shaped ice cubes, such as spheres, diamonds, and stars, or silicone baking molds.

Multi-layer ice cubes

Freeze ice cubes in layers of different colors or add elements to each layer. Wait for each layer to freeze before adding the next.

FROZEN FRUIT

Shape choices

Use frozen fruit to decorate and refresh cocktails. Use cookie cutters to make a variety of shapes, such as melon or watermelon balls, perfect for summer. Dice apples or pears and place them in an ice cube tray with the juice of the same fruit.

Choosing fruit

Choose fruit that goes well with your cocktail. Strawberries, raspberries, and blueberries, as well as citrus slices, are popular, especially if you grate them to get fresh zest.

FRESH, DRIED, CANDIED, CUT, OR WHOLE FRUITS AND VEGETABLES

There is a wide variety of fruits that can be used, depending on your creativity. Using fruit and vegetables in cocktails is a classic technique that can be visually appealing.

Wedges (apple, pear, peach, kiwi, apricot, citrus)

Cut ¼ or ⅛ of the fruit and make an incision to hang it over the rim of the glass, adding to the cocktail's aesthetic and aromatic profile. Apples and pears are a little more delicate than citrus fruits. The thickness of the rim will be a determining factor.

Fan (apple, pear, peach, cucumber)

Cut ⅓ of the apple into thin slices. Skewer them together at the bottom and open them up into a fan shape. Place at an angle on the rim of the glass. To keep them upright, add another skewer vertically. You can add a piece of fruit at the end.

Slices and wheels (banana, star fruit, cucumber, citrus fruits)

Whether raw, dried, or candied, slices are often placed on the rim of the glass with a small incision to hold them in place. They add their own balance of flavors, colors, and textures, allowing for customization according to the occasion or even the season.

Cut the slice into halves or quarters and place on an ice cube for a sophisticated presentation. As it melts, it subtly infuses the cocktail, offering an evolving taste experience. This method incorporates fruit without interfering with the taste.

Whole fruit (olive, cape gooseberry, blackcurrant, blackberry, raspberry, cherry, redcurrant)

Skewer the fruit and place it at the bottom of the glass or on top. It can also be placed on an ice cube, on the foam, or on the whipped cream.

PEEL

A popular decorative element for its fresh fragrance and beautiful, colorful appearance. Use without the white pith. Leave it raw, cut it neatly, twist it, roll it up, place it on the rim of the glass, or let it float on the surface. Once peeled with a vegetable peeler or a sharp knife, cut neatly to the desired length.

Lightly twist the peel over the glass to release its essential oils. Rub it on the rim to infuse the glass with its aroma. Rubbing the rim adds a bitter flavor to each sip. Running the peel around the base of the glass creates a subtle olfactory experience, transferring the aromas to your fingers for an immersive and enjoyable sensory experience.

The shape and size of the peel will vary according to cocktail style and preference. For a twisted peel, wrap it around a cylindrical object such as a chopstick.

The art of expressing

The technique of expressing oils involves pinching or twisting the peel over the cocktail to release its essential oils, a fine aromatic mist sometimes referred to in French as "absolut." Expressing the peel above the glass enriches the fragrant bouquet of the cocktail. This technique, often used for non-citrus drinks, stimulates the taste buds and tantalizes your nose before each sip.

HERBS

Rinsing fresh herbs in iced water before using them as a garnish enhances their appearance, making them brighter and fresher. This preserves their vibrant color and makes them stiffer, and therefore easier to handle. After immersion, gently shake or pat with paper towel to remove excess water. As well as enhancing the visual appeal, fresh herbs add a subtle aromatic dimension to the drink, making tasting more immersive and sensory.

Releasing their aromas

Often used to release the essential oils from herbs, this technique adds a fresh aroma and intensifies the drink. By gently tapping or clapping the herbs between your hands, you delicately break the cells without crushing or grinding them, thus avoiding bitterness and visual damage. The goal is to release the aromas without damaging the leaves. You should immediately smell a stronger aroma emanating from the herbs. If not, clap them again.

Placing a small bouquet of aromatic herbs near the straw enhances the tasting experience. As you drink, your nose is above the glass and you inhale the fresh aromas of the herbs. This proximity creates a multi-sensory experience, enriching the cocktail with herbal notes.

This is because our perception of taste is closely linked to our sense of smell. By integrating herbs in this way, you increase the aromatic complexity of the drink, making each sip even more delicious.

This is a very useful tip for cocktails where herbs play a key role in the flavor profile, such as juleps or mules with mint or basil. Not only does this enhance the taste experience, but it also adds an aesthetic element to the cocktail, making it more visually appealing.

GETTING A NICE FOAM

Emulsion is crucial for creating and stabilizing the foam in cocktails. Here's how it works and why it's essential for quality foam.

How it forms

Incorporating air: vigorously shaking a cocktail with emulsifiers (egg whites, aquafaba, certain liqueurs) incorporates air, creating bubbles surrounded by liquid, which form foam. Emulsifiers increase viscosity and stabilize the bubbles, allowing the foam to remain on the surface without dissipating quickly.

Its stability

- **Density:** the foam, less dense than the liquid, floats on the surface of the cocktail. For stable foam, it must be firm enough to resist dissolving in the liquid below.

- **Durability:** a well-emulsified, firm foam dilutes less quickly, keeping the pattern created with the bitters visible for longer. This is crucial in cocktails, where aesthetics are essential to the tasting experience.
- **Temperature:** cold cocktails maintain foam longer than hot drinks, as heat accelerates bubble dissolution.

In short, a well-executed foam enhances the aesthetics of the beverage and enriches the taste and sensory experience through its texture and the aromas released.

THE ART OF BITTERS

Adding a few drops of aromatic bitters or other light liquids to transform cocktails turns a simple drink into a visual and tasty work of art, just as some baristas do with coffee. This method adds elegance to the cocktail and introduces subtle aromatic nuances, enhancing the tasting experience. Use a cocktail pick or knife blade for this.

CARAMEL DECORATIONS

Caramel decorations add an artistic and elegant touch to cocktails, providing a sophisticated and original presentation that will impress your guests.

They can add a subtle sweetness to cocktails, balancing out bitter or acidic flavors. However, overcooked caramel can become bitter. Keep an eye on it while cooking and remove it from the heat as soon as it reaches the desired color and consistency.

1 - Melt sugar until it turns a golden-brown color.
2 - To make strands, dip a fork into the caramel and quickly pull the strands onto parchment paper.
3 - To make a shell, dip a ladle into the caramel and allow it to harden before peeling off.

PEARLS

Used in baking, sugar pearls add a luxurious touch. Available in a variety of colors, sizes, and flavors, they are made from crystallized sugar and can be coated with shiny or colored layers for a fun visual effect.

In cocktails, they add visual appeal and a crunchy texture. Place them on the rim of the glass or in the cocktail. They are popular with festive drinks, such as those served at weddings.

JELLY CUBES

Jelly cubes add color to cocktails. Make jelly with water, sugar, and gelatin (or agar-agar for a vegan version), adding fruit juices, flavorings, or colorings to suit the theme of the cocktail.

Once set, cut the jelly into cubes and add the cubes to the glass. The cubes can float, mix with the drink, or be used as a garnish on the rim of the glass for a fun visual and taste effect.

SPHERES

Spherification encapsulates your cocktail or one of its components in an edible sphere, surprising your guests when it bursts in the mouth.

1 – **Prepare the base solution:** mix the cocktail or component to be spherified with sodium alginate.
2 – **Prepare the reaction bath:** dissolve calcium chloride in water.
3 – **Form the spheres:** use a spoon or pipette to drop the alginate mixture into the calcium chloride bath. A syringe gives you precise control, ideal for creating uniform spheres.
4 – **Leave to react:** after a few seconds to a minute, a membrane forms around the drops, creating spheres.
5 – **Rinse and serve:** remove the spheres with a slotted spoon, rinse them gently with water, and add them to the cocktail for a flavor explosion in the mouth.

DRIED OR FRESH FLOWERS

Whether dried or fresh, flowers enhance the appearance and sometimes even the aroma of cocktails in an elegant, natural way.

Fresh flowers

- **Directly in the cocktail:** putting petals or whole flowers in the glass or on ice brings color, freshness, beauty, and sometimes a delicate scent.
- **On the rim of the glass:** attach a whole flower, with a small notch or petals, to decorate the rim of the glass with syrup.
- **In ice:** freeze small flowers in ice for a refreshing and unique presentation.

Dried flowers

Play with cocktail colors by delicately sprinkling dried flowers over the surface, especially on drinks with foam, for a natural, elegant visual effect.

Mix finely ground dried flowers with sugar or salt to create a beautiful rimming on the glass.

Cocktail decorations are essential to the tasting experience. They enhance aesthetics and introduce new textures and flavors, improving every sip. In this way, decoration goes beyond embellishment – it's an invitation to explore and appreciate the complexity and creativity of each glass.

COCKTAIL RECIPES

INTRODUCTION

The use of beer in cocktails is gaining in popularity, adding a new dimension to alcoholic beverages.

Using beer brings:

- **A huge variety of aromas:** beer offers a wide range of styles with unique profiles, from light and refreshing to complex and rich. Its various ingredients add nuances of aroma, texture, and taste, giving complexity and depth to cocktails, allowing customization with a large palette of flavors.
- **Sparkle:** the effervescence of beer adds texture, such as creaminess and an airy tone, making cocktails more refreshing and enjoyable to drink, especially on hot days.
- **Low alcohol content:** with a lower alcohol content than spirits, beer makes for lighter cocktails. It's ideal for those who want to enjoy a cocktail without feeling quickly intoxicated.
- **Versatility:** the immense diversity of beers is a major asset for bartenders, enabling them to experiment and innovate. Suitable for all seasons, they can be used for all types of cocktails, whether refreshing or comforting. The combinations are endless.
- **Tradition and innovation:** using beer in cocktails reflects centuries-old brewing traditions and mixology innovation. Bartenders often combine modern techniques with classic recipes to create new ones.

THE RECIPES

On the following pages, you'll find various beer styles and their attributes, to help you better understand their role in cocktails. Each introduction is followed by recipes specific to that style.

For each cocktail, you'll find the ingredients, equipment required, type of glass, and preparation method. Beer measurements are not given as they depend on your glass.

For fruit, juice is usually given as an alternative, but it is preferable to use fresh fruit in season.

SOUR BEER

Called sour beer by the Anglo-Saxons, these beers are characterized by a tart taste, high or spontaneous fermentation with ale yeast, lactic bacteria, wild yeast, or cultured yeast. Inspired by Belgian lambics, they capture natural yeasts and bacteria, creating unique, complex notes.

CHERRY ON TOP

GLASS TYPE: OLD FASHIONED

INGREDIENTS:

- 1 fl oz (30 ml) Armagnac Dry Cellar (Dartigalongue)
- 1 fl oz (30 ml) dark chocolate liqueur (Mozart)
- ⅓ fl oz (10 ml) cherry syrup (Monin)
- BEER: Duchesse de Bourgogne Chocolat Cherry (Verhaeghe Brewery)
- 1 square of dark chocolate
- 1 Amarena cherry
- Ice

EQUIPMENT

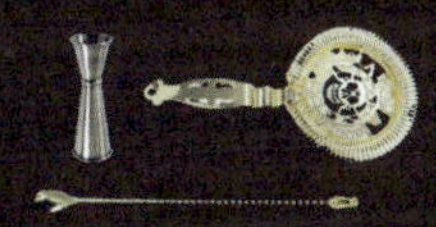

IN A MIXING GLASS

1 – Pour all ingredients into the shaker, except the beer and garnishes.

2 – Fill with ice and stir.

3 – Serve through a double strainer.

4 – Top with beer and stir.

5 – Garnish: a square of dark chocolate and an Amarena cherry.

MARGOTE

EQUIPMENT

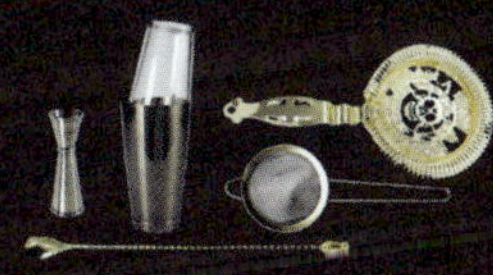

GLASS TYPE: TASTING

INGREDIENTS:

- 1⅓ fl oz (40 ml) vodka B42
- ⅔ fl oz (20 ml) Italicus
- ⅓ fl oz (10 ml) bergamot syrup (Monin)
- BEER: lemon sour
- 1 tbsp marmalade mix
- Citrus peel
- Ice

IN THE SHAKER

1 – Pour all the ingredients except the beer into the shaker and dissolve the marmalade.

2 – Fill shaker with ice and shake.

3 – Serve through a double strainer.

4 – Top with beer and stir.

5 – Garnish: citrus peel.

MALT ATTACK

GLASS TYPE: FANCY

INGREDIENTS:

- ⅔ fl oz (20 ml) white Adriatico
- 1 handful of raspberries (or 1 fl oz [30 ml] juice)
- ⅓ fl oz (10 ml) cane sugar syrup (Monin)
- BEER: Sour Acid Attack (1989 Brewery)
- Ice

IN THE SHAKER

1 – Reserving some for the garnish, mash a few raspberries in a shaker and add all the ingredients except the beer.

2 – Fill shaker with ice and shake.

3 – Serve through a double strainer.

4 – Top with beer and stir.

5 – Garnish: raspberry skewer.

SUNBURN

GLASS TYPE: COUPE

INGREDIENTS:

- $\frac{2}{3}$ fl oz (20 ml) Fable whisky
- $\frac{2}{3}$ fl oz (20 ml) plum-vanilla liqueur (Edinburgh)
- $\frac{1}{3}$ fl oz (10 ml) squeezed lemon juice
- BEER: Vanilla-strawberry sour
- Strawberries
- 1 wild garlic flower
- Ice

IN THE SHAKER

1 – Pour all ingredients into the shaker, except the beer and garnishes.

2 – Fill shaker with ice and shake.

3 – Serve through a double strainer.

4 – Top with beer and stir.

5 – Garnish: strawberry fan and a wild garlic flower.

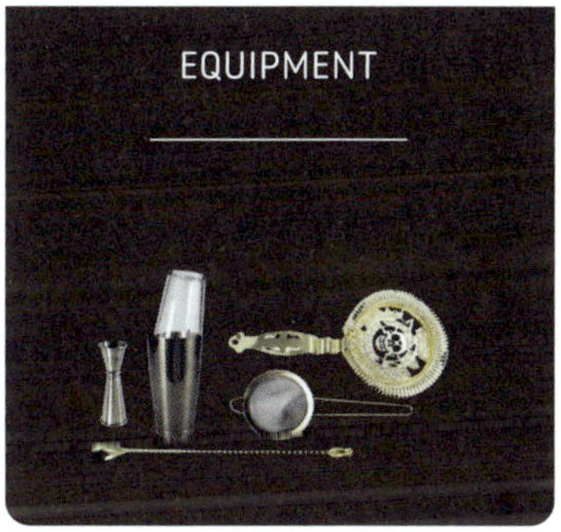

PINK BADASS

GLASS TYPE: TUMBLER

INGREDIENTS:

- 1 fl oz (30 ml) Bombay Bramble gin
- ⅔ fl oz (20 ml) cranberry syrup (Monin)
- ⅓ fl oz (10 ml) squeezed lemon juice
- BEER: Lush Berliner Weisse raspberry (Amundsen Brewery)
- 1 raspberry
- 1 blackberry
- Ice

IN THE SHAKER

1 – Pour all ingredients into the shaker, except the beer and garnish.

2 – Fill shaker with ice and shake.

3 – Serve through a double strainer.

4 – Top with beer and stir.

5 – Garnish: a raspberry and blackberry skewer.

TROPIC COLADA SOUR

GLASS TYPE: TUMBLER

INGREDIENTS:

- 1⅓ fl oz (40 ml) white rum (Eminente)
- 1 tbsp coconut cream
- A few pineapple pieces (or 1 fl oz [30 ml] pineapple juice)
- BEER: Sour Tropic Thunder (Dugges Brewery)
- 1 whole pineapple
- Ice

IN THE SHAKER

1 – Mash a few pineapple chunks in the shaker, add all the ingredients except the beer, and do an initial dry shake.

2 – Fill the shaker with ice and give it another shake.

3 – Serve over ice, double filtered.

4 – Top with beer and stir.

5 – Garnish: a piece of pineapple and two pineapple leaves.

EQUIPMENT

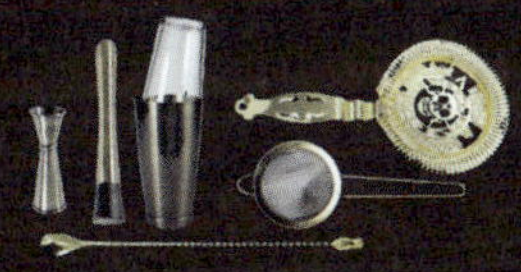

VOODOO CARNIVAL

GLASS TYPE: TIKI

DID YOU KNOW? Exotic cocktails have a long history, dating back to the 1930s and 1940s, when the United States became fascinated with faraway islands and tropical cultures. This craze symbolized adventure and escape to sunny destinations. Over the years, people have been drawn to tropical flavors and new taste experiences.

INGREDIENTS:

- ⅓ fl oz (10 ml) Gayuma dark rum (Don Papa)
- ⅓ fl oz (10 ml) Tricorn white rum (Compagnie des Indes)
- ⅓ fl oz (10 ml) yuzu liqueur (Choya)
- ⅔ fl oz (20 ml) Ancho Reyes Verde
- A few blood orange segments (or ⅔ fl oz [20 ml] juice)
- A few grapefruit segments (or 1 fl oz [30 ml] juice)
- ⅓ fl oz (10 ml) squeezed lemon juice
- BEER: sour-style with exotic fruits
- Basil
- 1 slice dried pineapple
- Pansies
- Ice

IN THE SHAKER

1 – Mash a few blood orange and grapefruit segments in a shaker, squeeze the basil and add all the ingredients except the beer and garnishes.

2 – Fill shaker with ice and shake.

3 – Serve over ice, double filtered.

4 – Top with beer and stir.

5 – Garnish: a slice of dried pineapple, pansies and basil.

MAI TAI TROPICAL SOUR

GLASS TYPE: OLD FASHIONED

INGREDIENTS:

- ⅔ fl oz (20 ml) dark rum Sherry Cask (Saison)
- ⅔ fl oz (20 ml) of a fruity, honeyed white rum
- ⅔ fl oz (20 ml) triple sec (Maison Ferrand)
- ⅓ fl oz (10 ml) squeezed lemon juice
- ½ fl oz (15 ml) orgeat syrup (Monin)
- 1 fl oz (30 ml) pineapple juice (optional)
- BEER: sour-style with exotic fruits
- a few pineapple pieces (or 1 fl oz [30 ml] juice)

EQUIPMENT

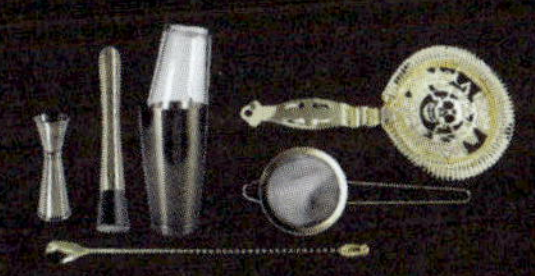

IN THE SHAKER

1 – Mash pineapple chunks in shaker, leaving some for garnish, add all ingredients except beer.

2 – Fill shaker with ice and shake.

3 – Serve over ice, double filtered.

4 – Top with beer and stir.

5 – Garnish: pineapple chunks and a pineapple leaf.

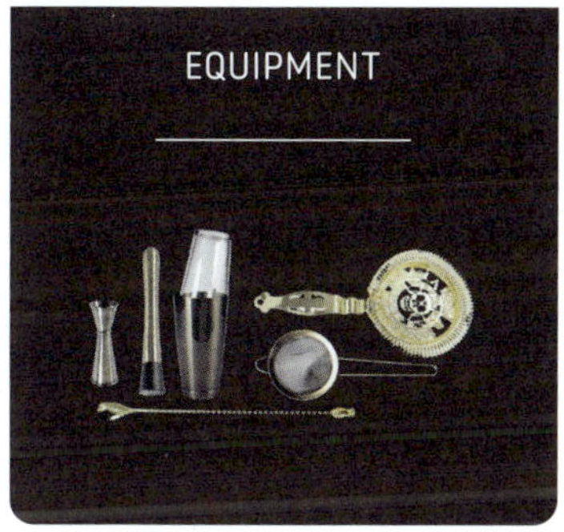

PUMP IT UP

GLASS TYPE: TASTING

INGREDIENTS:

- ⅔ fl oz (20 ml) Lone Wolf Raspberry gin (Brewdog) (optional)
- ⅓ fl oz (10 ml) jasmine syrup (Bacanha)
- BEER: Berliner Weiss beer with red berries or a sour beer with red berries
- A handful of raspberries (or 1 fl oz [30 ml] juice)
- A handful of cranberries (or 1⅓ fl oz [40 ml] juice)
- Ice

IN THE SHAKER

1 – Mash the fruit in a shaker and add all the ingredients except the beer.

2 – Fill shaker with ice and shake.

3 – Serve through a double strainer.

4 – Top with beer and stir.

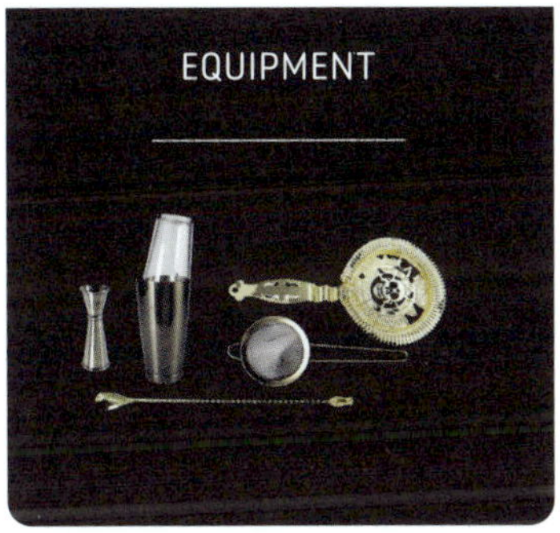

GREEK SIDE

GLASS TYPE: COUPE

INGREDIENTS:

- 1⅓ fl oz (40 ml) Votanikon gin
- ⅔ fl oz (20 ml) lemon juice
- ⅔ fl oz (20 ml) cane sugar syrup (Monin)
- BEER: cucumber-flavored Gose beer or infuse cucumber in the gin and use a classic Gose beer
- 1 cucumber slice
- Ice

IN THE SHAKER

1 – Pour all ingredients into the shaker, except the beer and garnish.

2 – Fill shaker with ice and shake.

3 – Serve through a double strainer.

4 – Top with beer and stir.

5 – Garnish: cucumber skewer.

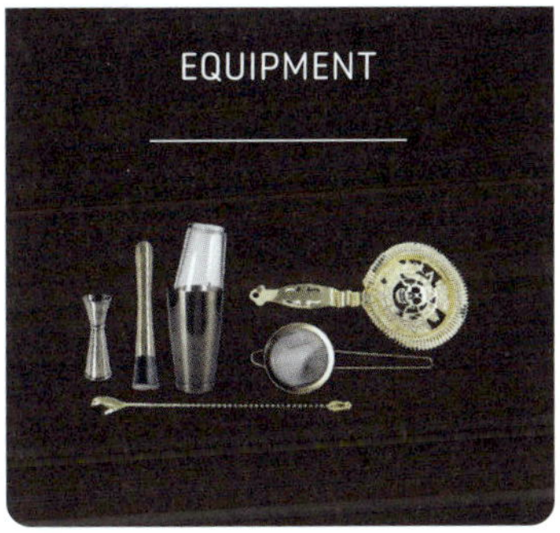

PINEAPPLE COVE

GLASS TYPE: TASTING

INGREDIENTS:

- 1⅓ fl oz (40 ml) Organic Coco white rum (Union)
- 1 fl oz (30 ml) Grand Marnier
- A few pieces of pineapple (or 1⅓ fl oz [40 ml] juice)
- ⅔ fl oz (20 ml) lemon juice
- 1 tbsp coconut cream
- BEER: Exotic fruits sour (with coconut, if possible)
- Ice

IN THE SHAKER

1 – Mash a few pineapple chunks in a shaker, then add all the ingredients except the beer.

2 – Do an initial dry shake.

3 – Fill with ice, shake it again.

4 – Serve through a double strainer.

5 – Top with beer and stir.

6 – Garnish: a coconut-dusted dried pineapple slice* and pineapple leaves.

*COCONUT PINEAPPLE SLICE:
As per the rimming technique, dip part of the slice in lemon juice, then in coconut shavings.

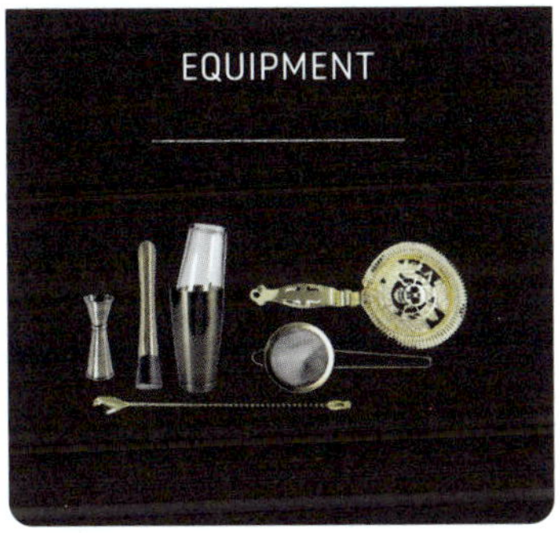

MEXICAN D'ARTAGNAN MULE

GLASS TYPE: METAL MUG

INGREDIENTS:

- 1 fl oz (30 ml) Abasolo whisky
- 1 fl oz (30 ml) Ley 925 tequila
- ⅔ fl oz (20 ml) ginger beer syrup
- 1 ripe cherimoya (or 1 fl oz [30 ml] juice)
- ⅓ fl oz (10 ml) lime juice
- BEER: Fruit Sour Guava Rodeo (Oscar Blues Brewery)
- Ginger slivers
- Dried lime wheel
- Crushed ice

IN THE SHAKER

1 – Make the cold syrup with the ginger beer (see page 64).

2 – Crush the cherimoya in a shaker and pour in all the ingredients except the beer and garnish.

3 – Fill shaker with ice and shake.

4 – Serve over crushed ice, double filtered.

5 – Top with beer and stir.

6 – Garnish: ginger slivers and a dried lime wheel.

COPPERY SUNSET

GLASS TYPE: OLD FASHIONED

INGREDIENTS:

- 1⅓ fl oz (40 ml) old plum (Maison Escagnan)
- 1 fl oz (30 ml) Guignolet d'Anjou liqueur
- 2 plums (or 1 fl oz [30 ml] juice)
- ⅓ fl oz (10 ml) white peach syrup (Monin)
- 1 dash Fee Brothers peach bitter
- BEER: a sour classic

EQUIPMENT

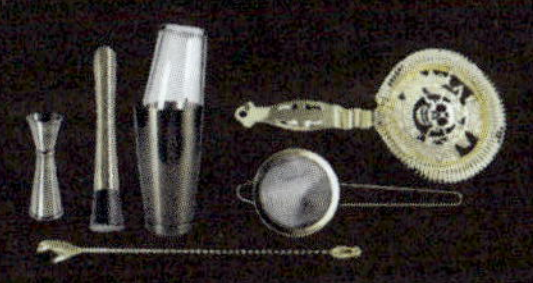

IN THE SHAKER

1 – Reserving a wedge for garnish, mash a few pieces of plum in a shaker, then add all the ingredients except the beer.

2 – Fill shaker with ice and shake.

3 – Serve through a double strainer.

4 – Top with beer and stir.

5 – Garnish: a plum wedge.

BLUE VELVET

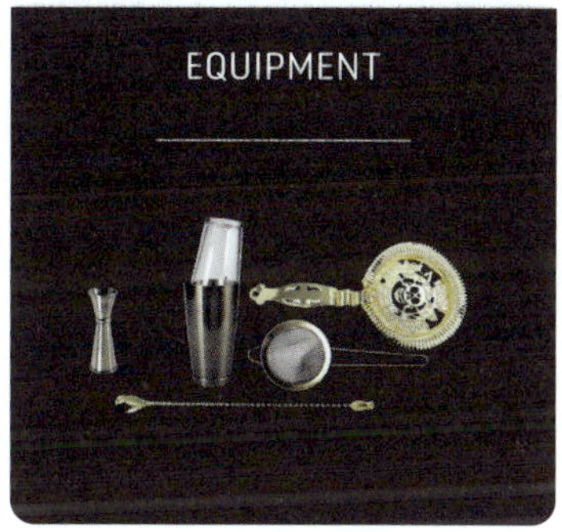

GLASS TYPE: FANCY

INGREDIENTS:

- 1⅓ fl oz (40 ml) Boatyard vodka
- ½ fl oz (15 ml) blueberry syrup (Monin)
- ½ fl oz (15 ml) lemon juice
- 1 dash cherry bitter (Fee Brothers)
- BEER: Sour Berry Good (Pohjala Brewery)
- A handful of blueberries (or 1 fl oz [30 ml] blueberry juice)
- A few borage flowers
- Ice

IN THE SHAKER

1 – Reserving some for the garnish, mash blueberries in shaker, pour in all ingredients except beer and flowers.

2 – Fill shaker with ice and shake.

3 – Serve over ice, double filtered.

4 – Top with beer and stir.

5 – Garnish: a skewer of blueberries and some borage flowers.

CHARLENE SOUR

GLASS TYPE: OLD FASHIONED

INGREDIENTS:

- ⅔ fl oz (20 ml) La Gauloise jaune
- ⅔ fl oz (20 ml) amaretto (Quaglia)
- 1 fl oz (30 ml) lemon juice
- ⅓ fl oz (10 ml) poppy syrup (Des Lis)
- BEER: a cherry or thyme-flavored Gose-style beer, or a classic sour beer
- 1 egg white
- Rosemary leaves
- Amarena cherries
- Ice

EQUIPMENT

IN THE SHAKER

1 – Pour all the ingredients into the shaker, except the beer and garnishes, and do an initial dry shake.

2 – Fill with ice, then shake it again.

3 – Serve through a double strainer.

4 – Top with beer and stir.

5 – Garnish: a few rosemary leaves and a skewer of Amarena cherries.

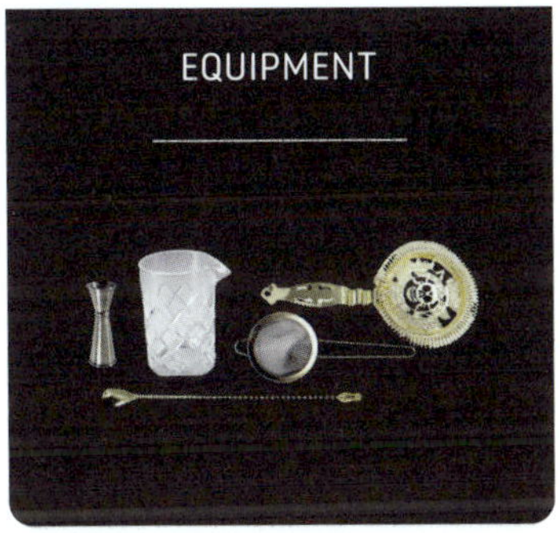

ABYSS CANDY

GLASS TYPE: MARTINI

INGREDIENTS:

- 1 fl oz (30 ml) Empress 1908 gin
- 1 fl oz (30 ml) fruit salad juice
- ⅓ fl oz (10 ml) cotton candy syrup (Monin)
- ½ fl oz (15 ml) lemon juice
- BEER: peach sour
- Cotton candy (Cakelicious)
- Ice

IN A MIXING GLASS

1 – Put a little cotton candy in the bottom of the glass, reserving some for garnish.

2 – Put ice on top, pour all ingredients except the beer into the mixing glass and stir.

3 – Serve through a double strainer.

4 – Top with beer and stir.

5 – Garnish: cotton candy.

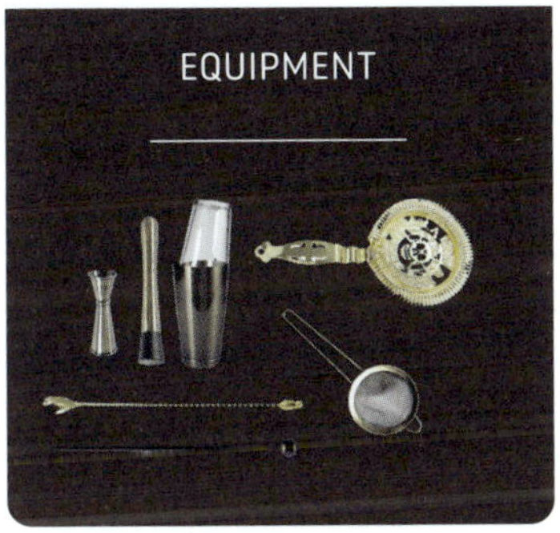

PURPLE IN LOVE

GLASS TYPE: TASTING

INGREDIENTS:

- 1⅓ fl oz (40 ml) Tamboo Spiced dark rum (Angostura)
- ⅔ fl oz (20 ml) triple sec (Giffard)
- A handful of blackberries (or 1 fl oz [30 ml] juice)
- ⅓ fl oz (10 ml) blackberry syrup (Monin)
- BEER: Berliner Weiss with strawberries or red berries
- 1 egg white
- Sugar
- Ice

IN THE SHAKER

1 – Rim the glass with blackberry syrup and sugar.

2 – Reserving two for garnish, mash the blackberries in a shaker and pour in all the ingredients except the beer.

3 – Fill shaker with ice and shake.

4 – Serve through a double strainer.

5 – Top with beer and stir.

6 – Garnish: a blackberry skewer.

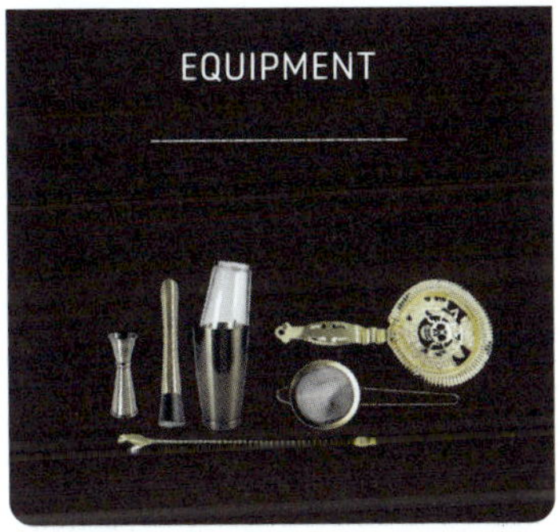

JUICY JUNGLE

GLASS TYPE: BOSTON

INGREDIENTS:

- 1⅓ fl oz (40 ml) dark rum no. 12 (Botran)
- A few pieces of pineapple (or 1 fl oz [30 ml] juice)
- ½ fl oz (15 ml) passion fruit syrup (Monin)
- 1 tbsp coconut cream
- BEER: Sour Mango (Dugges Brewery)
- 1 slice of starfruit
- Mint leaves
- 1 piece of pineapple
- Ice

IN THE SHAKER

1 – Mash a few pineapple chunks in the shaker, add all the ingredients except the beer and garnishes and do an initial dry shake.

2 – Fill with ice, then shake it again.

3 – Serve through a double strainer.

4 – Top with beer and stir.

5 – Garnish: a piece of pineapple, a slice of starfruit and mint leaves.

EQUIPMENT

SOUR POPPINO

GLASS TYPE: COUPE

DID YOU KNOW? Frozen cocktails are icy, refreshing drinks, often made with fruit, liqueurs, and crushed ice blended until smooth. Perfect for summer, they offer a vibrant, thirst-quenching tasting experience.

INGREDIENTS:

- 1 fl oz (30 ml) Lind & Lime gin
- ⅔ fl oz (20 ml) of a light lemon-infused aperitif or limoncello
- ⅔ fl oz (20 ml) limoncello (Mamma Mia)
- ⅓ fl oz (10 ml) mandarin syrup (Monin)
- BEER: Orange Gose (Pohjala Brewery)
- 1 or 2 scoops of orange sorbet
- 1 clementine

IN A MIXING GLASS

1 – Place the glass and the clementine in the freezer.

2 – Grate the frozen clementine into the bottom of the glass, reserving some for garnish.

3 – Pour all ingredients except beer and sorbet into mixing glass and stir.

4 – Add orange sorbet as needed, then whisk until the mixture is smooth but not too runny.

5 – Empty into the glass and top with beer.

6 – Garnish: reserved grated clementine and thinly sliced peel.

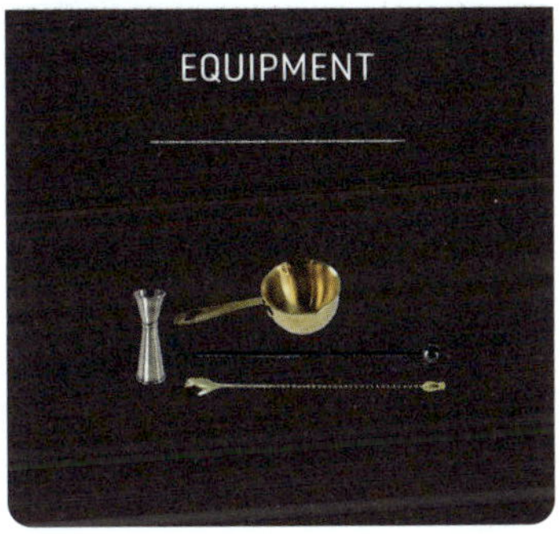

TO MY LOVE

GLASS TYPE: TODDY

INGREDIENTS:

- 1⅓ fl oz (40 ml) Naga Malacca rum
- 1 fl oz (30 ml) Suprême walnut liqueur (Denoix)
- ⅔ fl oz (20 ml) tiramisu syrup (Monin)
- 1 espresso
- BEER: Kriek cuvée René (Lindemans Brewery)
- Amarena cherries
- 1 candied orange slice

BUILD IN THE GLASS

1 – Heat the beer without bringing it to the boil, add the tiramisu syrup and stir.

2 – Warm the glass in hot water.

3 – Pour in all ingredients except beer and garnishes and stir.

4 – Top with beer and stir.

5 – Garnish: Amarena cherry skewer and a slice of candied orange.

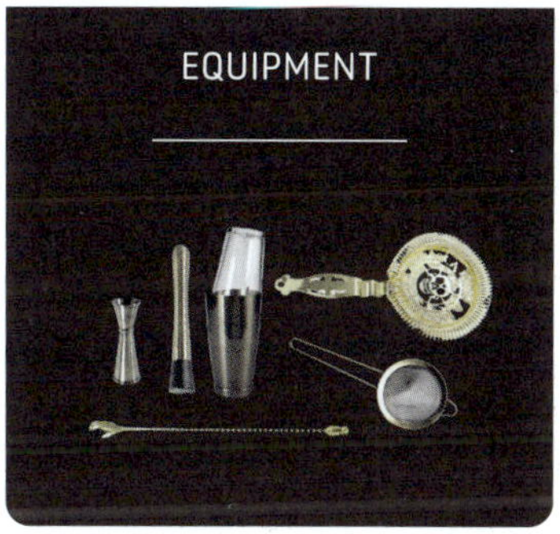

TROPICOOL

GLASS TYPE: FANCY

INGREDIENTS:

- 1⅓ fl oz (40 ml) dark rum Reserve (Saison)
- ⅓ fl oz (10 ml) Fernet-Branca
- ⅓ fl oz (10 ml) spiced red fruit syrup (Monin)
- A few pieces of pineapple (or 1⅓ fl oz [40 ml] juice)
- 1 handful of raspberries (or 1 fl oz [30 ml] juice)
- 1 tbsp coconut cream
- BEER: red fruits Imperial Pastry Sour
- Ice

IN THE SHAKER

1 – Reserving a few raspberries for garnish, mash the fruit in a shaker and pour in all the ingredients except the beer.

2 – Fill shaker with ice and shake.

3 – Serve through a double strainer.

4 – Top with beer and stir.

5 – Garnish: a raspberry skewer and pineapple leaves.

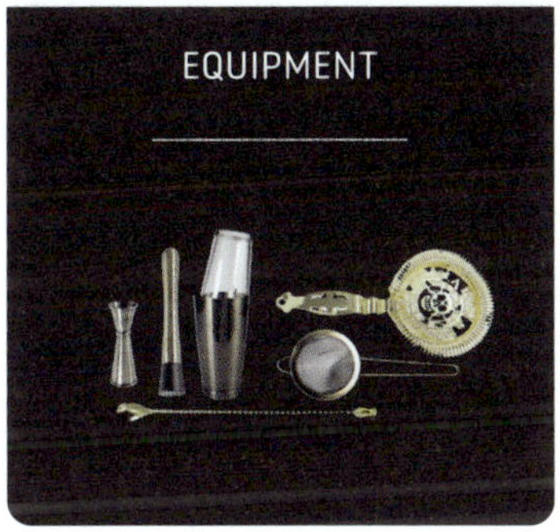

WO PINK

GLASS TYPE: TEA GLASS

INGREDIENTS:

- 1⅓ fl oz (40 ml) red gin (Citadelle)
- ⅓ fl oz (10 ml) Vincent Apéritif
- ⅓ fl oz (10 ml) lingonberry syrup (Monin)
- BEER: Sour Black Currant (Dugges Brewery)
- 1 handful of blueberries (or 1 fl oz [30 ml] juice)
- 1 egg white
- Lemon peel
- Dried lingonberries
- Ice

IN THE SHAKER

1 – Mash the blueberries in a shaker, pour in all the ingredients except the beer and garnishes and do an initial dry shake.

2 – Fill with ice, then shake it again.

3 – Serve through a double strainer.

4 – Top with beer and stir.

5 – Garnish: lemon peel and dried lingonberries.

EQUIPMENT

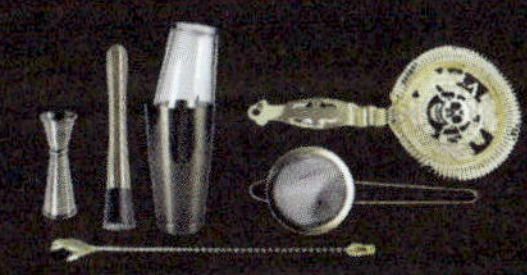

MILLIONAIRE 37

GLASS TYPE: TASTING

INGREDIENTS:

- 1 fl oz (30 ml) Original whisky (Arlette)
- ⅔ fl oz (20 ml) Grand Marnier
- 1 tsp absinthe (Pontarlier Cousin Jeune)
- A few apricot pieces (or 1⅓ fl oz [40 ml] juice)
- ⅓ fl oz (10 ml) grenadine syrup (Monin)
- BEER: apricot sour
- 1 egg white
- Ice
- ½ grilled apricot

IN THE SHAKER

1 –Mash a few apricot pieces in a shaker, pour in all the ingredients except the beer and garnish, and do an initial dry shake.

2 – Fill with ice, then shake it again.

3 – Serve through a double strainer.

4 – Top with beer and stir.

5 – Garnish: ½ grilled apricot.

EQUIPMENT

ADAM & EVE

GLASS TYPE: TASTING

INGREDIENTS:

- 1 fl oz (30 ml) 6-year-old calvados (Coquerel)
- 1 fl oz (30 ml) spiced dark rum (Compagnie des Indes)
- A few apple pieces (or 1⅔ fl oz [50 ml] juice)
- ⅓ fl oz (10 ml) pineapple syrup (Monin)
- BEER: Apple (Lindemans Brewery)
- 1 egg white
- Caramel chips

IN THE SHAKER

1 – Rim the glass with the pineapple syrup and caramel chips.

2 – Reserving some for garnish, mash a few apple pieces in the shaker, pour in all the ingredients except the beer and do an initial dry shake.

3 – Fill with ice, shake it again.

4 – Serve through a double strainer.

4 – Top with beer and stir.

6 – Garnish: caramel rim and an apple “leaf.”

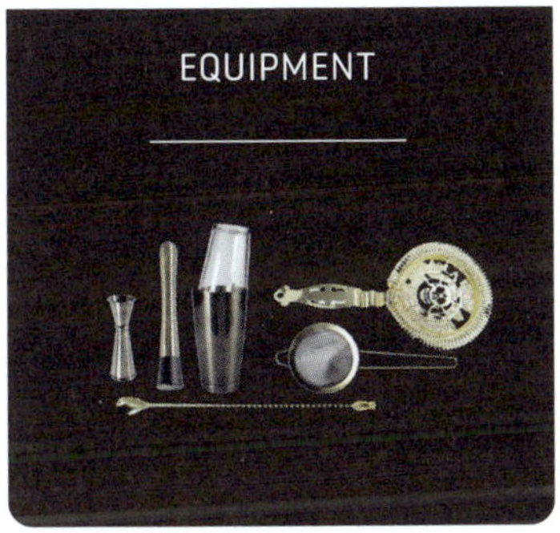

GREEN BERMUD'ALE DEVIL

GLASS TYPE: TUMBLER

INGREDIENTS:

- 1⅓ fl oz (40 ml) 6-year-old dark rum (Demon Share)
- ⅔ fl oz (20 ml) blue curaçao (Giffard)
- A few pieces of pineapple (or 1⅓ fl oz [40 ml] juice)
- ⅓ fl oz (10 ml) squeezed lemon juice
- ⅔ fl oz (20 ml) coconut water
- ⅓ fl oz (10 ml) rosemary syrup (Bacanha)
- BEER: Sun City (Pohjala Brewery)
- 1 egg white
- Coconut shavings
- Mint leaves
- Ice

IN THE SHAKER

1 – Rim the glass with rosemary syrup and coconut shavings.

2 – Mash a few pineapple chunks in the shaker, pour in all the ingredients except the beer and mint and do an initial dry shake.

3 – Fill with ice, shake it again.

4 – Serve through a double strainer.

4 – Top with beer and stir.

6 – Garnish: coconut rim and mint leaves.

RED REFLECTION

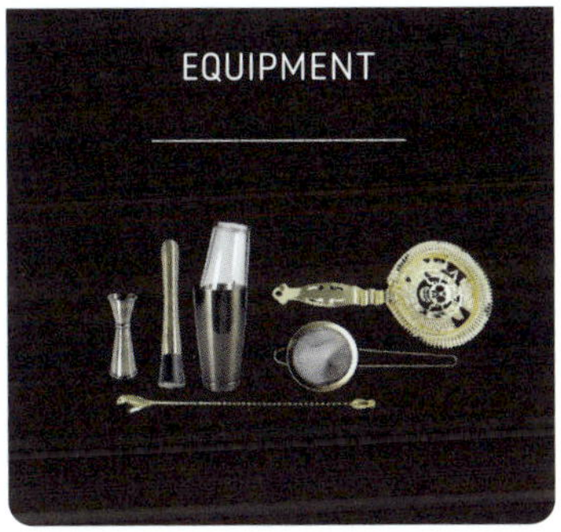

GLASS TYPE: TASTING

INGREDIENTS:

- 1⅓ fl oz (40 ml) Mohn gin
- ⅔ fl oz (20 ml) rhubarb liqueur (Giffard)
- A handful of raspberries (or 1⅓ fl oz [40 ml] juice)
- ⅓ fl oz (10 ml) squeezed lemon juice
- ⅓ fl oz (10 ml) raspberry syrup (Monin)
- BEER: strawberry and peach sour, or a peach or strawberry sour
- 1 egg white
- Pink pralines, crushed
- Rhubarb strips
- Ice

IN THE SHAKER

1 – Rim glass with raspberry syrup and crushed pralines.

2 – Reserving some for garnish, place the rhubarb strips in the glass.

3 – Mash the raspberries in the shaker, pour in all the ingredients except the beer and do an initial dry shake.

4 – Fill with ice, then shake it again.

5 – Serve through a double strainer.

6 – Top with beer and stir.

7 – Garnish: praline rim and rhubarb strips.

EQUIPMENT

NAUTIC'ALE

GLASS TYPE: BOSTON

INGREDIENTS:

- 1⅓ fl oz (40 ml) Transatlantic gin (Bordeaux Distilling)
- 1 apricot (or ⅔ fl oz [20 ml] juice)
- ⅓ fl oz (10 ml) squeezed lemon juice
- ⅓ fl oz (10 ml) raspberry syrup (Monin)
- BEER: apricot Gose or apricot sour
- 1 egg white
- Lilac sugar flowers (Cakelicious)
- 1 snapdragon
- Ice

IN THE SHAKER

1 – Mash the apricot in a shaker, pour in all the ingredients except the beer and garnishes, and do an initial dry shake.

2 – Fill with ice, then shake it again.

3 – Serve through a double strainer.

4 – Top with beer and stir.

5 – Garnish: lilac Cakelicious sugar flowers and a snapdragon.

MINT CHOCOBEET RUM

GLASS TYPE: OLD FASHIONED

SIGNATURE COCKTAIL – CESAR DEBUS

INGREDIENTS:

- 1 fl oz (30 ml) 3 Stars white rum (Plantation)
- ½ fl oz (15 ml) lime juice
- ⅓ fl oz (10 ml) chocolate syrup (Monin)
- BEER: beetroot Gose or sour
- 2 squares of dark chocolate
- Mint leaves
- Ice

IN THE SHAKER

1 – Pour all ingredients into the shaker, except the beer and garnishes.

2 – Fill shaker with ice and shake.

3 – Top with beer and stir.

4 – Garnish: two squares of dark chocolate and mint leaves.

WHEAT BEER AND FRUITY WHEAT BEER

Wheat beers, cloudy and unfiltered, are known for their freshness and natural sweetness. Whether in Germany, Belgium, or the United States, each country brings its own unique touch. Weissbier, rich in esters, evokes banana and cloves, while Witbier is distinguished by coriander and bitter orange peel, offering a spicy profile. American Wheat Beer is less yeasty, with hoppy tones and floral and fruity notes. Light and subtly tart, these refreshing beers appeal to a wide range of palates.

LUCKY SAMURAI

GLASS TYPE: TEA GLASS

INGREDIENTS:

- 1⅔ fl oz (50 ml) Fuyu whisky
- ⅔ fl oz (20 ml) Nihonshu Junmai sake
- ½ fl oz (15 ml) jasmine syrup (Bacanha)
- 1 persimmon (or 1⅓ fl oz [40 ml] juice)
- ⅔ fl oz (20 ml) lemon juice
- BEER: Hitachino Nest (Kiuchi Brewery)
- 1 edible wafer dahlia
- Ice

EQUIPMENT

IN THE SHAKER

1 – Mash a few pieces of persimmon in a shaker, then pour in all the ingredients except the beer and garnish.

2 – Fill shaker with ice and shake.

3 – Serve through a double strainer.

4 – Top with beer and stir.

5 – Garnish: edible wafer dahlia.

EQUIPMENT

MISTY SEA AROUND THE ISLAND

GLASS TYPE: BOSTON

INGREDIENTS:

- 1 fl oz (30 ml) Pointe Blanche whisky
- 1 fl oz (30 ml) dark rum XO (Plantation)
- A few pieces of pineapple (or 1⅓ fl oz [40 ml] juice)
- 1 mango (or 1⅓ fl oz [40 ml] juice)
- ⅔ fl oz (20 ml) lime juice
- ⅓ fl oz (10 ml) muscovado syrup (Monin)
- 1⅔ fl oz (50 ml) cold-brewed coffee
- BEER: a citrus wheat beer, preferably lemon flavored
- Black nonpareils
- Mint leaves
- Ice

IN THE SHAKER

1 – Rim the glass with black nonpareils.

2 – Make a cold-brew coffee.

3 – Reserving a slice of pineapple for garnish, mash the fruit in the shaker, pour in all the ingredients except the beer and mint.

4 – Fill shaker with ice and shake.

5 – Serve through a double strainer.

6 – Top with beer and stir.

7 – Garnish: black nonpareils rim, ½ pineapple slice and mint leaves.

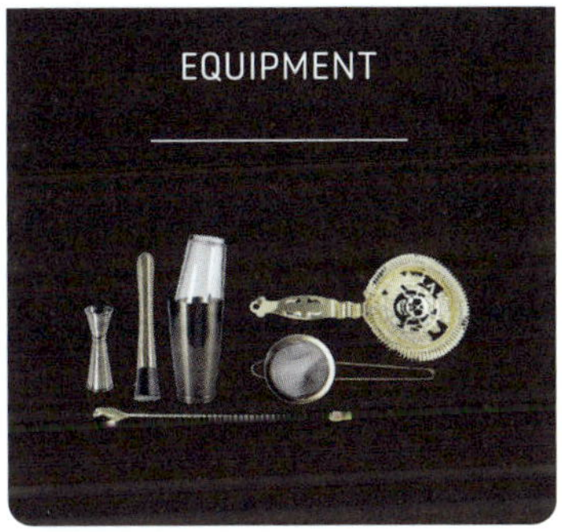

GREEN DIOSA

GLASS TYPE: OLD FASHIONED

INGREDIENTS:

- 1⅓ fl oz (40 ml) silver tequila (Diego & Maria)
- ⅔ fl oz (20 ml) lemon juice
- ½ fl oz (15 ml) honey syrup (Monin)
- BEER: a Gose-style beer with cucumber or infuse cucumber in the tequila and use a classic sour beer such as Berliner Weiss.
- A few mint leaves, plus extra for garnish
- 1 cucumber
- Ice

IN THE SHAKER

1 – Slice thin strips of cucumber and, leaving one for garnish, press them against the inside of the glass, using the ice to hold them in place.

2 – Squeeze out the mint leaves, crush a few pieces of cucumber in a shaker and add all the ingredients except the beer.

3 – Fill shaker with ice and shake.

4 – Serve through a double strainer.

4 – Top with beer and stir.

6 – Garnish: a thin slice of cucumber and mint leaves.

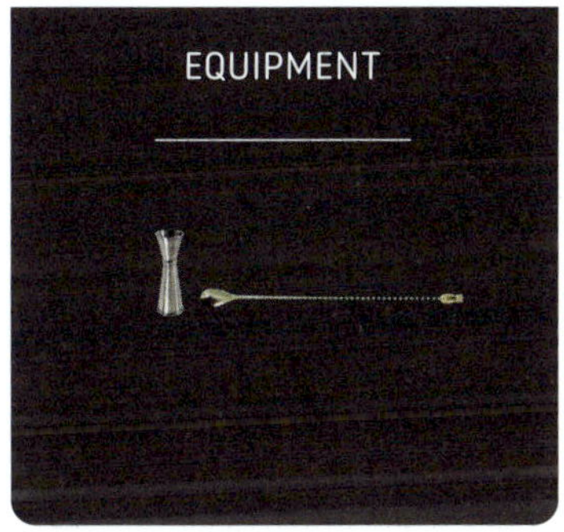

PINK REFRESHER

GLASS TYPE: TASTING

INGREDIENTS:

- 1⅓ fl oz (40 ml) Zealots gin (Brewdog Brewery)
- ⅔ fl oz (20 ml) violet liqueur (Giffard)
- BEER: Pink Killer (De Sully Brewery)
- Violet candies
- Dried flowers

IN THE SHAKER

1 – Crush violet candies to rim the glass with the violet liqueur.

2 – Pour in all ingredients except beer and garnish and stir.

3 – Top with beer and stir.

4 – Garnish: violet candy rim and dried flowers.

BASIL INSTINCT

GLASS TYPE: OLD FASHIONED

EQUIPMENT

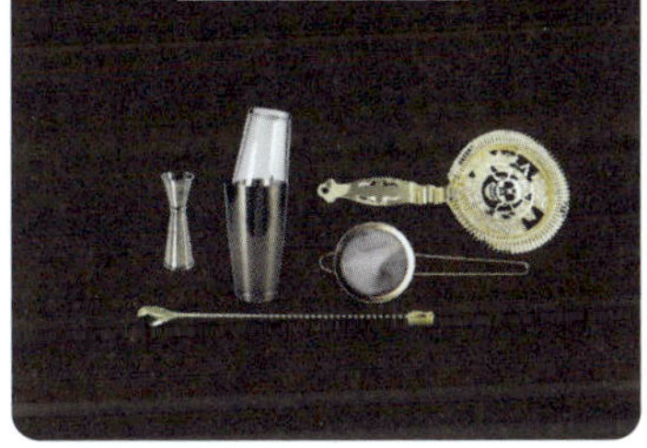

INGREDIENTS:

- 1⅓ fl oz (40 ml) Santa Ana gin
- ⅔ fl oz (20 ml) crème de menthe (Ernest)
- ⅔ fl oz (20 ml) lime juice
- ⅓ fl oz (10 ml) basil syrup (Monin)
- BEER: a wheat beer (white beer) with basil
- Mint leaves
- Purple basil leaves
- Lime peel
- Ice

IN THE SHAKER

1 – Reserving some for garnish, bruise and finely chop the basil and mint leaves.

2 – Place all the ingredients except the beer and garnishes in the shaker.

3 – Fill shaker with ice and shake.

4 – Serve through a double strainer.

5 – Top with beer and stir.

6 – Garnish: lime peel, mint and purple basil leaves.

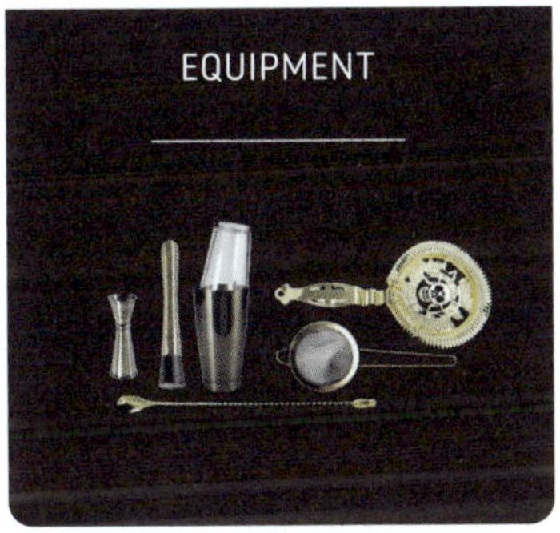

BEER PORN MARTINI

GLASS TYPE: MARTINI

DID YOU KNOW? The "Porn star Martini" was previously known as the "Maverick Martini." It became popular for its bold character and elegant presentation. For the Beer Porn Martini, the mix of sweet and tart, combined with the effervescent touch provided by the beer, makes for a delightfully charming cocktail. What's more, its provocative name and accompanying beer shooter contribute to its elegance and appeal to customers looking for a memorable experience.

INGREDIENTS:

- 1⅓ fl oz (40 ml) vanilla vodka (Absolut)
- 1 passion fruit (or 1 fl oz [30 ml] fruit juice), plus extra ½ passion fruit for garnish
- A few pieces of pineapple (or 1 fl oz [30 ml] juice)
- ⅓ fl oz (10 ml) passion fruit syrup (Monin)
- BEER: an exotic fruits sour beer
- Ice

IN THE SHAKER

1 – Mash a few pieces of pineapple and passion fruit in a shaker, then add all the ingredients except the beer.

2 – Fill shaker with ice and shake.

3 – Serve through a double strainer.

4 – Top with beer and stir, serve with a shot of beer on the side.

5 – Garnish: ½ passion fruit and a shot of beer.

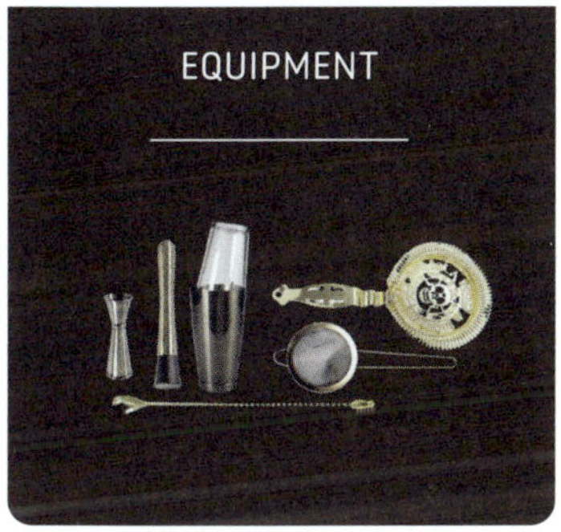

SUMMER SPLASH

GLASS TYPE: TASTING

INGREDIENTS:

- 1⅓ fl oz (40 ml) Houblon vodka (Aroc Bows)
- 1 fl oz (30 ml) watermelon liqueur (Giffard)
- ⅓ fl oz (10 ml) lime syrup (Monin)
- BEER: Blanche La Trappe (La Trappe Brewery)
- A few pieces of watermelon (or 2 fl oz [60 ml] juice)
- Mint leaves
- Crushed ice

IN THE SHAKER

1 – Reserving some for garnish, mash a few pieces of watermelon in a shaker, then pour in all the ingredients except the beer and mint leaves.

2 – Fill shaker with ice and shake.

3 – Serve over crushed ice, filtering twice.

4 – Top with beer and stir.

5 – Garnish: watermelon slice and mint leaves.

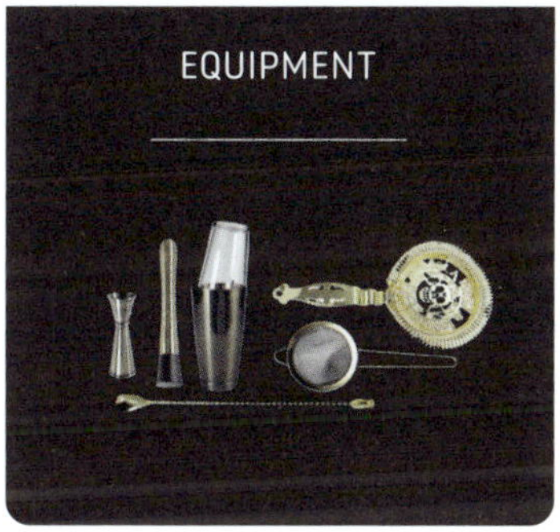

ULYSSES 41

GLASS TYPE: BOSTON

INGREDIENTS:

- 1⅓ fl oz (40 ml) fruity, floral, spicy gin
- ⅔ fl oz (20 ml) honey syrup (Monin)
- 1 fl oz (30 ml) lemon juice
- A few pieces of watermelon (or 2 fl oz [60 ml] juice)
- BEER: a wheat beer (white beer) with raspberry
- 1 pinch of pepper
- Ice

IN THE SHAKER

1 – Macerate peppercorns in honey syrup for 24 hours (optional).

2 – Reserving a slice for garnish, mash a few pieces of watermelon in a shaker, then pour in all the ingredients except the beer and pepper.

3 – Fill shaker with ice and shake.

4 – Serve through a double strainer.

5 – Top with beer and stir, add a pinch of pepper.

6 – Garnish: watermelon slice.

STRONG ALE

These are very diverse beers, known for their high effervescence, which varies according to origin, alcohol content and complex aroma profiles. They often have fruity, spicy and alcoholic tones, offering a rich experience. Enjoyed for their ability to combine richness and drinkability, they are popular for festive meals, celebrations and relaxing evenings. Some are relatively bitter and rather malty, with notes of caramel, hazelnut, cooked fruit (apple, pear) and dried fruit (fig, raisin), reminiscent of certain desserts. This category stands out for its complexity.

RUSTIC MULE

GLASS TYPE: MULE MUG

SIGNATURE COCKTAIL – LAURENCE MAROT

INGREDIENTS:

- 1⅓ fl oz (40 ml) Navy Strength Cannonball Edinburgh gin
- ⅔ fl oz (20 ml) lime juice
- ½ fl oz (15 ml) ginger syrup (Bacanha)
- 1 tsp sugar syrup
- BEER: a Tripel-style beer
- Lime peel
- Beetroot chips
- Crushed ice

IN THE SHAKER

1 – Pour all ingredients except beer and garnishes into shaker.

2 – Fill shaker with ice and shake.

3 – Serve over crushed ice, filtering twice.

4 – Top with beer and stir.

5 – Garnish: lime peel and beetroot chips.

SERENADE

GLASS TYPE: OLD FASHIONED

INGREDIENTS:

- 1 fl oz (30 ml) Altess dark rum (Maison Mairot)
- 1 fl oz (30 ml) The Botanist gin
- ½ fl oz (15 ml) raspberry syrup (Monin)
- A handful of raspberries (or 1 fl oz [30 ml] juice)
- ½ fl oz (15 ml) lime juice
- BEER: a Tripel-style beer aged in rum barrels
- Mint leaves
- Ice

EQUIPMENT

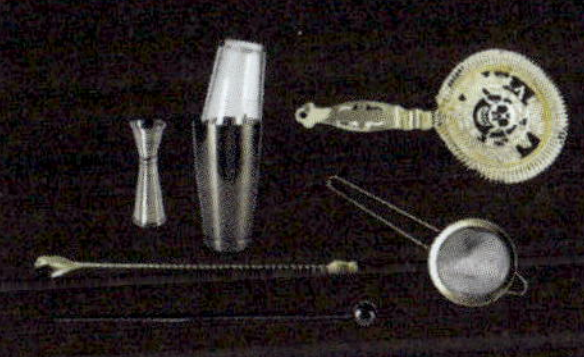

IN THE SHAKER

1 – Reserving some for garnish, mash the raspberries in a shaker and pour in all the ingredients except the beer and garnishes.

2 – Fill shaker with ice and shake.

3 – Serve through a double strainer.

4 – Top with beer and stir.

5 – Garnish: a raspberry skewer and mint leaves.

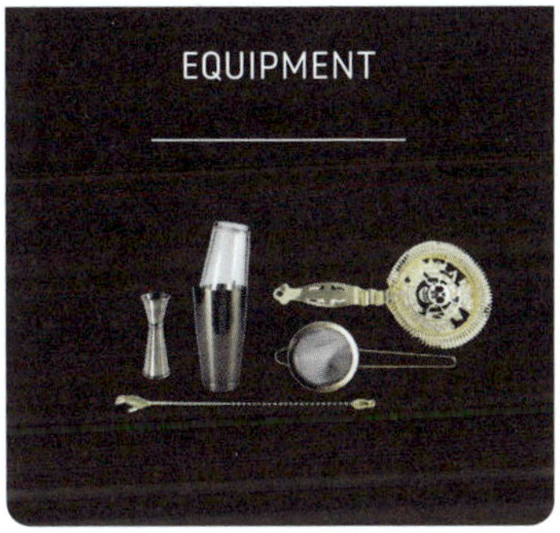

GOOD FORTUNE

GLASS TYPE: TASTING

INGREDIENTS:

- 1 fl oz (30 ml) Jurançon calvados (Maison Groult)
- ⅔ fl oz (20 ml) West Indies rum (Compagnie des Indes)
- 1 tsp vanilla syrup (Monin)
- 1 tsp liquid caramel
- BEER: Malheur brut (De Landtsheer Brewery)
- 1 tsp salted butter caramel
- 1 apple
- Ice

IN THE SHAKER

1 – Caramelize a few apple slices and steep them in the calvados for 12 hours.

2 – Filter the calvados.

3 – Place all the ingredients except the beer in the shaker.

4 – Fill shaker with ice and shake.

5 – Serve through a double strainer.

6 – Top with beer and stir.

7 – Garnish: caramelized dried apple chips.

GARDEN OF EDEN

GLASS TYPE: TASTING

INGREDIENTS:

- 1⅓ fl oz (40 ml) Santiago de Cuba 8-year-old dark rum
- A few apple pieces (or 1 fl oz [30 ml] juice)
- ⅔ fl oz (20 ml) lemon juice
- ⅔ fl oz (20 ml) apple tart syrup (Monin)
- 1 dash hibiscus syrup (Monin)
- BEER: a Belgian Strong Blond Ale
- 1 apple
- 1 candied hibiscus flower
- Ice

IN THE SHAKER

1 – Caramelize a few apple slices and steep them in the rum for 24 hours.

2 – Strain the rum, crush a few pieces of apple and then add all the ingredients except the beer and garnishes to the shaker.

3 – Fill shaker with ice and shake.

4 – Serve through a double strainer.

5 – Top with beer and stir.

6 – Garnish: a slice of apple and a candied hibiscus flower.

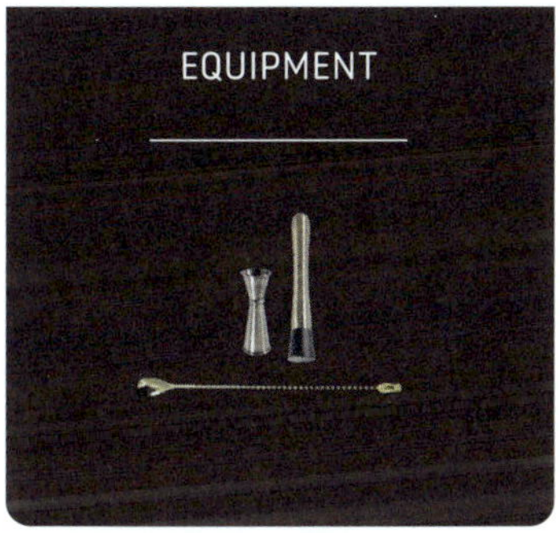

BAHIA SAMBA

GLASS TYPE: TEA GLASS

INGREDIENTS:

- 1 fl oz (30 ml) Ypióca Cachaça
- ⅔ fl oz (20 ml) sugar syrup
- BEER: St-Feuillien Grand Cru (St-Feuillien Brewery)
- 1 lime
- Crushed ice

BUILD IN THE GLASS

1 - Set aside a few lime wedges for the garnish and crush the rest with the syrup then add the Ypióca Cachaça.

2 - Fill with crushed ice, top with beer and stir.

3 - Garnish: lime wedges.

HARMONY

GLASS TYPE: NORA

EQUIPMENT

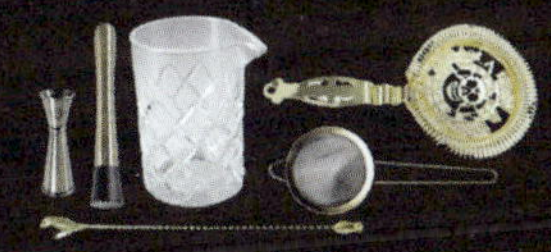

INGREDIENTS:

- 1⅓ fl oz (40 ml) single malt whisky with rich, pastry-like notes of vanilla, brioche, and pear
- 1 fl oz (30 ml) white vermouth (Jsotta)
- ⅓ fl oz (10 ml) mandarin syrup (Monin)
- 1 dash grapefruit bitters (Fee Brothers)
- BEER: Wee Heavy style
- 1 mandarin
- Ice

IN A MIXING GLASS

1 –Reserving some peel for garnish, mash the mandarin in the mixing glass and add all the ingredients except the beer and bitters.

2 – Fill with ice and stir.

3 – Serve through a double strainer.

4 – Top with beer, add a few drops of bitters, stir.

5 – Garnish: mandarin peel.

SPECIALTY BEERS

This category includes beers with added flavors, natural or otherwise, such as fruit, spices, chocolate, or other ingredients not used in traditional brewing. Specialty beers involve some form of modification of "classic" beers, either by the addition of extra ingredients (yeast/bacteria, smoke, wood, fruit, spices, grain, or sugar), or by an alternative process.

CRÈME BRÛLÉE

GLASS TYPE: COUPE

INGREDIENTS:

- 1⅓ fl oz (40 ml) vanilla vodka (Absolut)
- 1 fl oz (30 ml) crème de cacao (Giffard)
- 1⅔ fl oz (50 ml) old rum cream (Longueteau)
- ⅓ fl oz (10 ml) crème brûlée syrup (Monin)
- 2⅓ fl oz (70 ml) white chocolate sauce
- BEER: a pastry-style bock beer with hints of amaretto or almond
- 3 rows of chocolate
- Crème brûlée style caramel shell and tuile
- Ice

EQUIPMENT

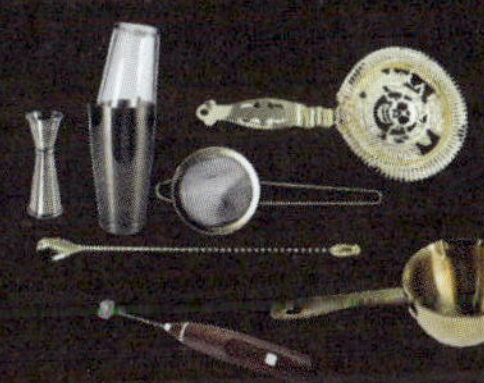

IN THE SHAKER

1 – Make 2⅓ fl oz (70 ml) of white chocolate sauce: heat 5 fl oz (150 ml) of milk and the 3 rows of chocolate for 20 minutes.

2 – Use a milk frother to remove the carbonation from the beer or simply let it go flat.

3 – Pour all the ingredients except the garnishes into the shaker and do an initial dry shake.

4 – Fill with ice, then shake it again.

5 – Serve through a double strainer.

6 – Garnish: crème brûlée style caramel shell and tuile.

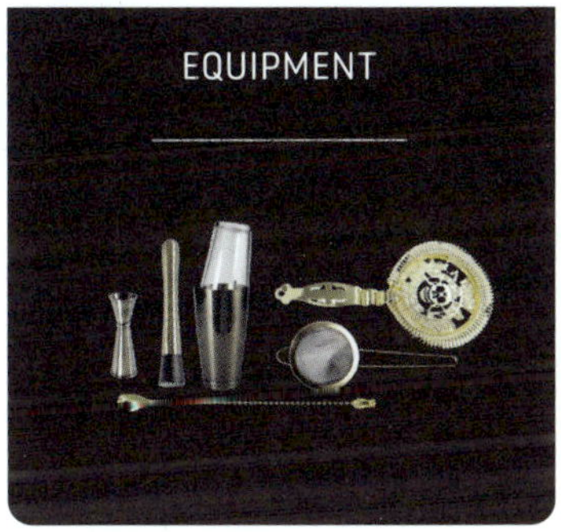

NERII TREASURE

GLASS TYPE: TASTING

INGREDIENTS:

- 1⅓ fl oz (40 ml) white rum with fruity notes of lychee and citrus
- 1 red kiwi (or 1 fl oz [30 ml] juice)
- ⅓ fl oz (10 ml) kiwi syrup (Monin)
- BEER: a pineapple Wild Sour-style beer
- 1 egg white
- Ice

IN THE SHAKER

1 –Reserving a slice for the garnish, mash a few pieces of red kiwi in a shaker, then add all the ingredients except the beer.

2 – Fill shaker with ice and shake.

3 – Serve through a double strainer.

4 – Top with beer and stir.

5 – Garnish: kiwi slice.

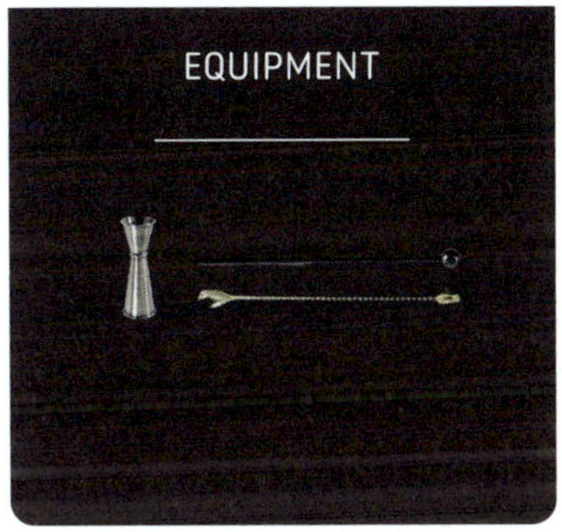

DARK MULE

GLASS TYPE: MULE MUG

INGREDIENTS:

- 1⅓ fl oz (40 ml) dark rum (Kong)
- 2 fl oz (60 ml) bergamot tonic or simple tonic
- ⅔ fl oz (20 ml) lime juice
- BEER: an extra dry ginger sour-style beer
- A few pieces of candied ginger
- Crushed ice
- Mint leaves

BUILD IN THE GLASS

1 – Reserving some for the garnish, express the mint.

2 – Fill glass with crushed ice, pour in all ingredients except beer and garnish and stir.

3 – Top with tonic, then beer, and stir.

4 – Garnish: skewer of candied ginger pieces and mint leaves.

AI AI AI!

GLASS TYPE: OLD FASHIONED

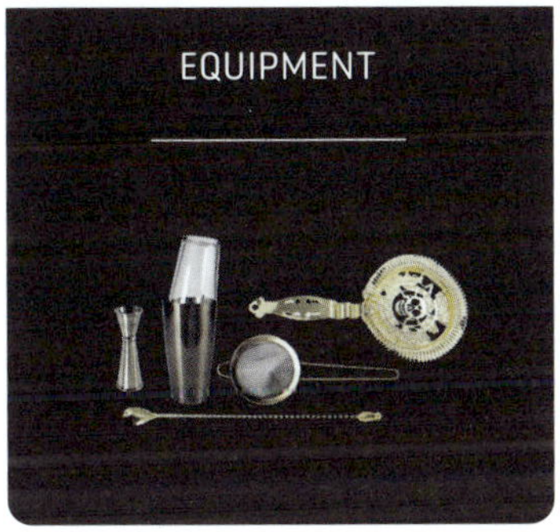

INGREDIENTS:

- 1⅓ fl oz (40 ml) Pig's Nose whisky
- ⅓ fl oz (10 ml) Gauloise verte
- BEER: a black garlic amber ale, or use black garlic paste with an amber ale
- ½ mixing spoon black garlic paste
- 1 garlic clove
- Ice

IN THE SHAKER

1 – Mix all the ingredients in the shaker, except the beer and garlic clove, using the milk frother to dissolve the black garlic paste.

2 – Fill shaker with ice and shake.

3 – Serve through a double strainer.

4 – Top with beer and stir.

5 – Garnish: a strip of garlic peel and a clove of black garlic.

EQUIPMENT

THIRSTY DANDY

GLASS TYPE: WINE GLASS

INGREDIENTS:

- ⅓ fl oz (10 ml) VSOP cognac Virgin Oak (Planat)
- ⅓ fl oz (10 ml) cherry liqueur (Heering)
- ⅓ fl oz (10 ml) mirabelle plum syrup (Monin)
- BEER: Old Tom Cat ginger (Robinson Brewery)
- Mint leaves
- Ice

IN A MIXING GLASS

1 – Pour all ingredients except beer and mint into mixing glass.

2 – Fill with ice and stir.

3 – Serve over ice, double filtered.

4 – Top with beer and stir.

6 – Garnish: mint leaves.

OLD FASHIONED CHOCOPEANUT

GLASS TYPE: OLD FASHIONED

INGREDIENTS:

- 1⅔ fl oz (50 ml) peanut-infused Wiseman bourbon
- ⅓ fl oz (10 ml) sugar syrup
- 1 dash Peychaud bitters
- BEER: a Pale Ale with cacao
- Peanuts
- 1 ice cube

FOR THE CHOCOLATE PEANUT BALL

- 1 cup of peanut butter
- ½ cup softened butter
- 2 cups powdered sugar
- ½ tsp vanilla extract
- 2 cups chocolate chips

IN A MIXING GLASS

1 – Mash peanuts and steep in whisky for 24 hours.

2 – Place an ice cube in the mixing glass, strain the whisky and then pour in all the ingredients except the beer and bitters.

3 – Stir and serve through a double strainer.

4 – Top with beer, add a dash of bitters and stir.

5 – Garnish: chocolate-covered peanut ball*.

*CHOCOLATE-COVERED PEANUT BALL:

Mix peanut butter, softened butter, powdered sugar and vanilla extract until smooth. Shape the dough into balls, and place on a baking sheet. Refrigerate for 45 minutes. Melt the chocolate chips. Coat peanut butter balls with melted chocolate. Leave to cool until the chocolate has hardened, then use a toothpick to hold the ball in place.

IPA, PALE ALE, AND AMERICAN PALE ALE

These beers are well known for their varying degrees of bitterness, high hop content, and complex aromatic notes that can include hints of citrus, flowers, resin, herbs, tropical fruits, or stone fruits, depending on the hop varieties used. Discover the different cocktails that can be made with these beers.

TROPICAL CRUSH

GLASS TYPE: BOSTON

SIGNATURE COCKTAIL – ROMEU MARTINS

INGREDIENTS:

- 2 fl oz (60 ml) Pink Pepper gin (Audemus)
- ⅔ fl oz (20 ml) lime juice
- ⅔ fl oz (20 ml) pink berry syrup
- BEER: Double Milkshake King Crush IPA (Brewdog Brewery)
- Mint leaves
- Pink berries
- Pineapple chunks
- Ice

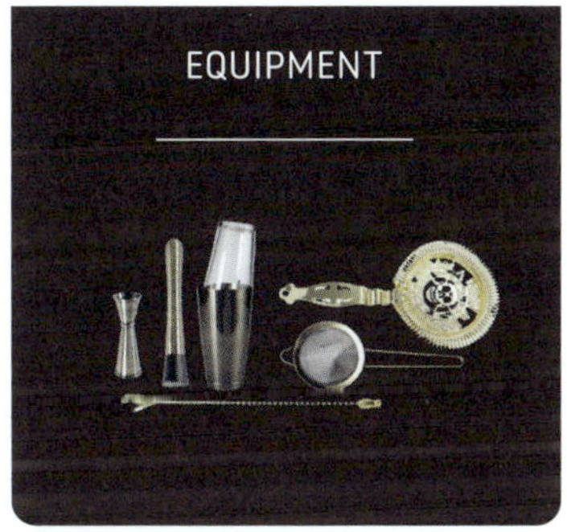

IN THE SHAKER

1 – Crush pink berries, then rim the glass with the syrup and berries.

2 – Add all the ingredients except the beer and garnishes to the shaker.

3 – Fill shaker with ice and shake.

4 – Serve over ice, double filtered.

5 – Top with beer and stir.

6 – Garnish: pink berries rimming, mint leaves and pineapple pieces.

EQUIPMENT

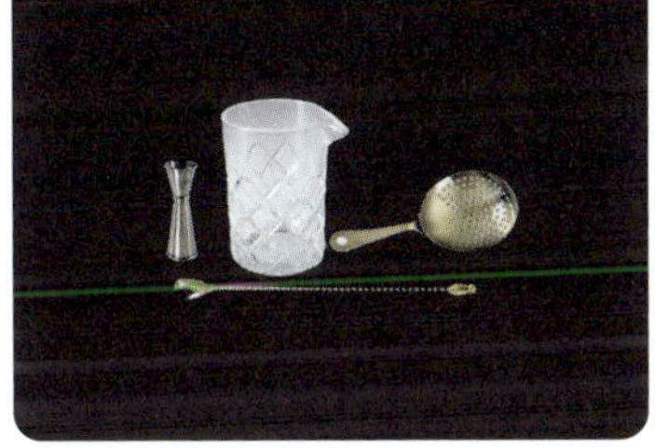

MINT HOP JULEP

GLASS TYPE: JULEP TUMBLER

INGREDIENTS:

- 1⅓ fl oz (40 ml) gin with citrus notes
- ⅔ fl oz (20 ml) beer brandy
- ⅔ fl oz (20 ml) tonic
- BEER: Neck Oil Session IPA (Beavertown Brewery)
- Mint leaves
- Lemon peel
- Crushed ice

BUILD IN THE GLASS

1 – Make a cold syrup with the tonic.

2 – Reserving some for the garnish, express the mint leaves.

3 – In the mixing glass, muddle the mint leaves with the syrup, then pour in the remaining ingredients, except beer and garnishes.

4 – Fill the glass with crushed ice.

5 – Serve through a double strainer.

6 – Top with beer and stir.

7 – Garnish: mint leaves and lemon peel.

EQUIPMENT

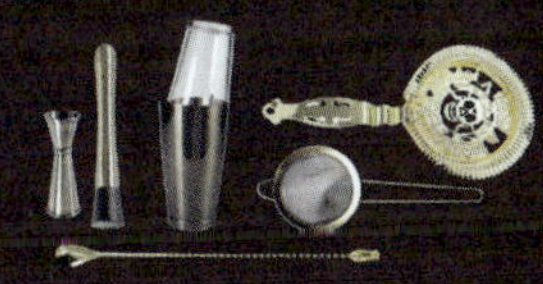

CARNIVAL

GLASS TYPE: OLD FASHIONED

INGREDIENTS:

- 1⅓ fl oz (40 ml) Z44 Special Edition gin (Roner)
- ⅔ fl oz (20 ml) lychee liqueur (Giffard)
- ⅓ fl oz (10 ml) verbena liqueur
- 1 dash Angostura bitter
- A few lychees (or 1⅓ fl oz [40 ml] juice)
- ⅔ fl oz (20 ml) lemon juice
- A little strawberry syrup (Monin)
- BEER: Water & Vuur NEIPA (De Molen Brewery)
- 1 snapdragon
- Ice

IN THE SHAKER

1 – Make flower-shaped ice cubes with a little strawberry syrup.

2 – Reserving 1 for the garnish, mash the lychees in a shaker and pour in all the ingredients except the beer and garnish.

3 – Fill shaker with ice and shake.

4 – Serve through a double strainer.

5 – Top with beer and stir.

6 – Garnish: a lychee, an ice cube with red fruit syrup and spices and a snapdragon.

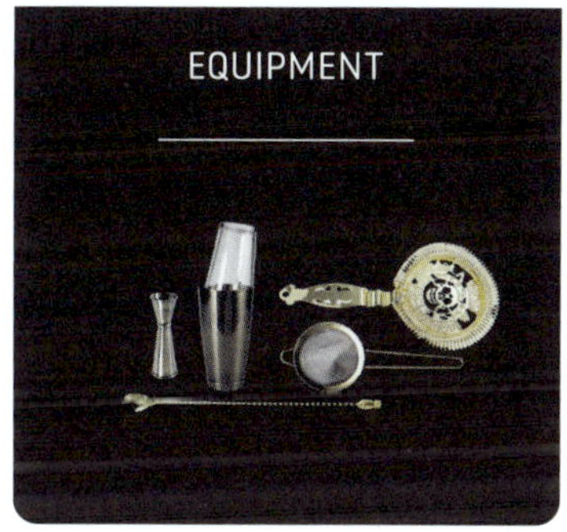

MEETING

GLASS TYPE: LARGE COUPE

SIGNATURE COCKTAIL – MATTHIAS GIROUD

DID YOU KNOW? When beer meets mixology and the flavors of France meet those of Belgium. A simple yet complex alcohol-free experience. Enjoy it on your own, with family or friends.

INGREDIENTS:

- A few pieces of apple (or 2 fl oz [60 ml] of juice infused with toasted buckwheat)
- ⅓ fl oz (10 ml) verjuice
- ½ fl oz (15 ml) salted caramel syrup (Monin)
- BEER: alcohol-free Belgian Blond Ale
- Buckwheat seeds
- Ice

IN THE SHAKER

1 – Reserving some for the garnish, mash the apple pieces and strain the juice.

2 – In an airtight jar, place the buckwheat in the apple juice just after toasting, and seal immediately. Leave to infuse cold for 12 to 18 hours, then double-strain. Store in a cool place before use.

3 – Place all the ingredients except the beer in the shaker.

4 – Fill shaker with ice and shake.

5 – Serve through a double strainer.

6 – Top with beer and stir.

7 – Garnish: slice apples into strips, sprinkle with sugar, caramelize with a blowtorch (optional) and cut into rosettes.

EQUIPMENT

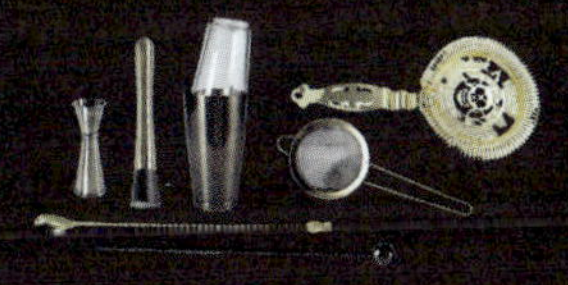

LYCHEE LULLABY

GLASS TYPE: TASTING

INGREDIENTS:

- 1⅓ fl oz (40 ml) Sherry Cask gin (Mr Gaston)
- ⅔ fl oz (20 ml) St-Germain
- ½ fl oz (15 ml) Noilly Prat
- ¾ fl oz (25 ml) lemon juice
- ⅓ fl oz (10 ml) lavender syrup (Monin)
- A few lychees (or 2 fl oz [60 ml] juice)
- BEER: Fancy Papers Hazy IPA (Cigar City Brewery)
- Nasturtiums
- 1 egg white
- Ice

IN THE SHAKER

1 –Reserving some for the garnish, mash the lychees in a shaker, pour in all the ingredients except the beer and nasturtiums and do an initial dry shake.

2 – Fill with ice, then shake it again.

3 – Serve through a double strainer.

4 – Top with beer and stir.

5 – Garnish: skewer of lychees and nasturtiums.

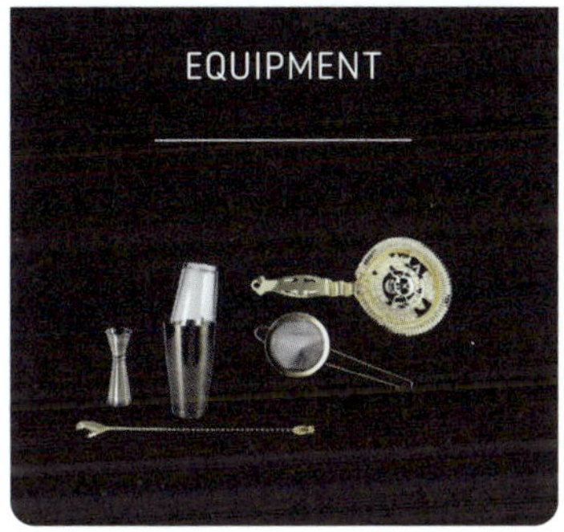

CHEEKY

GLASS TYPE: OLD FASHIONED

INGREDIENTS:

- 1 fl oz (30 ml) Napoleon mandarin juice
- ⅔ fl oz (20 ml) lemon juice
- ½ fl oz (15 ml) cane sugar syrup (Monin)
- BEER: Session IPA (Mousse de Rouergue Brewery)
- Mandarin peel
- Mandarin fruit paste
- Mint leaves
- Ice

IN THE SHAKER

1 – Pour all ingredients into the shaker, except the beer and garnish.

2 – Fill shaker with ice and shake.

3 – Serve over ice, double filtered.

4 – Top with beer and stir.

5 – Garnish: mandarin peel, mandarin fruit paste and mint leaves.

POLAR PALOMA

GLASS TYPE: LARGE COUPE

INGREDIENTS:

- 1 fl oz (30 ml) gin with resinous, citrus, and spicy notes
- 1 fl oz (30 ml) tequila Blanco (Kah)
- ⅔ fl oz (20 ml) agave syrup (Monin)
- BEER: a NEIPA style
- 2 candied orange wheels
- 2 scoops of grapefruit sorbet

BUILD IN THE GLASS

1 – Place the glass in the freezer.

2 – Pour all ingredients into the blender, except for the beer and garnish, blend and pour into the glass.

3 – Top with beer, stir.

4 – Garnish: candied orange wheels.

BRAMBLES

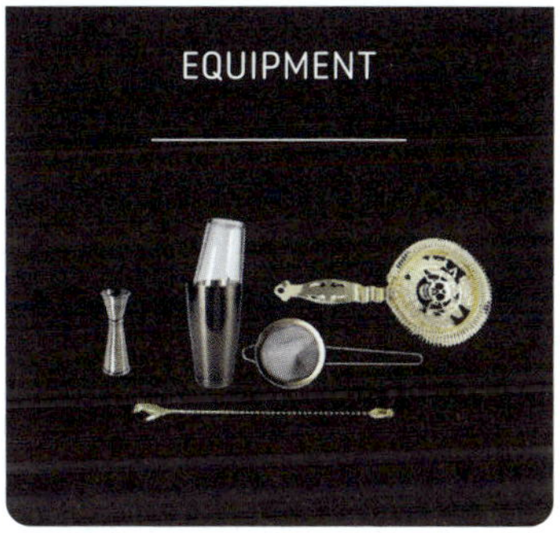

GLASS TYPE: TASTING

INGREDIENTS:

- 1⅓ fl oz (40 ml) Saigon Baigur gin
- ⅓ fl oz (10 ml) white bitters (Red)
- A few lychees (1⅓ fl oz [40 ml] juice)
- ⅔ fl oz (20 ml) lemon juice
- ⅔ fl oz (20 ml) blackberry syrup (Monin)
- Granulated sugar
- BEER: Jungle Joy (Brussel Beer Project Brewery)
- Lemon zest
- Ice

IN THE SHAKER

1 – Rim the glass with blackberry syrup and sugar.

2 – Reserving some for the garnish, mash the lychees in a shaker and add all the ingredients except the beer and zest.

3 – Fill shaker with ice and shake.

4 – Serve over ice, double filtered.

5 – Top with beer and stir.

6 – Garnish: lychee and lemon zest.

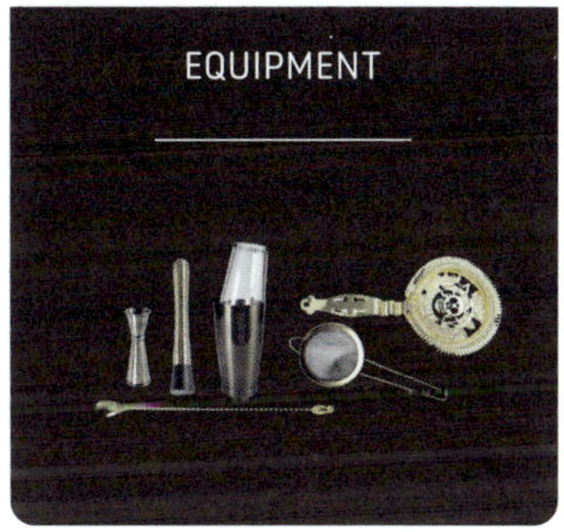

ROSY RIVIERA

GLASS TYPE: NORA

INGREDIENTS:

- 1⅓ fl oz (40 ml) Zest gin (Mermaid)
- 1 fl oz (30 ml) Bellecour bitters (Bigallet)
- A few grapefruit segments (or 2 fl oz [60 ml] juice)
- ⅓ fl oz (10 ml) squeezed lemon juice
- ⅔ fl oz (20 ml) pineapple syrup (Monin)
- BEER: Chill Time (Nuka Brewery)
- ½ slice pineapple
- Ice

IN THE SHAKER

1 – Mash a few grapefruit segments and add all the ingredients except the beer and garnish to the shaker.

2 – Fill shaker with ice and shake.

3 – Serve over ice, double filtered.

4 – Top with beer and stir.

5 – Garnish: ½ pineapple slice.

EQUIPMENT

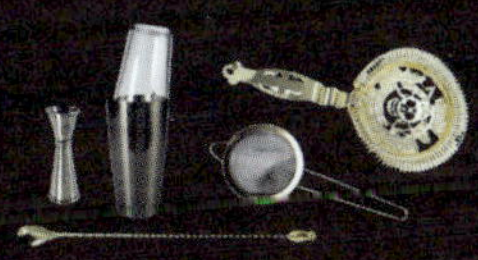

PASSIONATELY

GLASS TYPE: FLUTE

INGREDIENTS:

- 1⅓ fl oz (40 ml) Porter's Tropical Gin
- ½ passion fruit (or 1 fl oz [30 ml] juice), plus another ½ for garnish
- ⅓ fl oz (10 ml) lime syrup (Monin)
- BEER: Session IPA
- 2 vanilla pods

IN THE SHAKER

1 – Pour all ingredients into the shaker, except the beer and garnishes.

2 – Fill shaker with ice and shake.

3 – Serve through a double strainer.

4 – Top with beer and stir.

5 – Garnish: two vanilla pods and ½ passion fruit.

EQUIPMENT

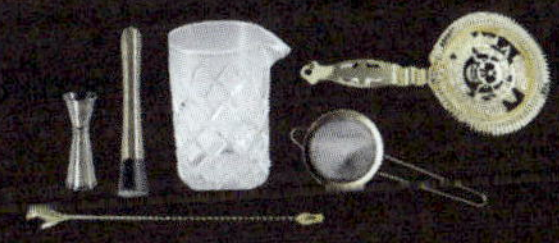

INFINITO

GLASS TYPE: FLUTE

INGREDIENTS:

- 1⅓ fl oz (40 ml) Cane Spirit dark rum (Lyre's)
- A few pieces of guava (or ⅔ fl oz [20 ml] juice)
- BEER: Alcohol-free IPA
- Ice

IN A MIXING GLASS

1 – Reserving some for the garnish, mash a few guava pieces in a mixing glass, add the rum and ice and stir.

2 – Serve through a double strainer.

3 – Top with beer and stir.

4 – Garnish: ½ slice guava.

EQUIPMENT

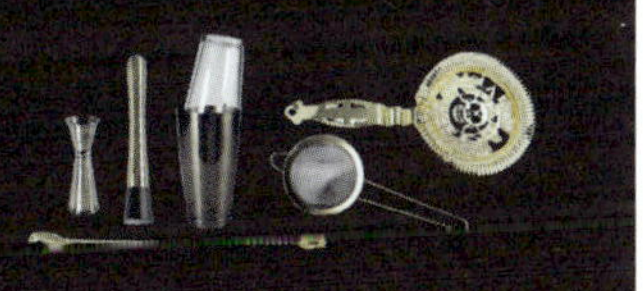

IMPERIAL

GLASS TYPE: LARGE COUPE

INGREDIENTS:

- 1 fl oz (30 ml) Naga Siam 12-year-old dark rum
- 1 fl oz (30 ml) a spicy, herby gin
- 1 tsp absinthe (Pontarlier Cousin jeune)
- A few pieces of pineapple (or 1 fl oz [30 ml] juice)
- 1 apple (or 1 fl oz [30 ml] juice)
- ⅓ fl oz (10 ml) squeezed lemon juice
- ⅓ fl oz (10 ml) lemongrass syrup (Monin)
- BEER: Wingman Session IPA (Brewdog Brewery)
- 1 orange peel
- Ice

IN THE SHAKER

1 – Mash the pineapple and apple pieces in a shaker, then add all the ingredients except the beer and garnish.

2 – Fill shaker with ice and shake.

3 – Serve over ice, double filtered.

4 – Top with beer and stir.

5 – Garnish: orange peel.

EQUIPMENT

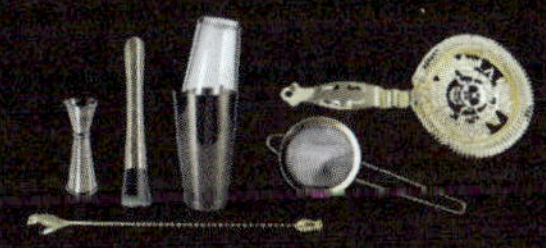

CELEBRATION

GLASS TYPE: NORA

INGREDIENTS:

- 1⅓ fl oz (40 ml) blanco tequila (Espolon)
- ⅔ fl oz (20 ml) vermouth (Del Professore)
- A few grapefruit segments (or 1⅔ fl oz [50 ml] juice)
- ⅓ fl oz (10 ml) lemon juice
- ⅓ fl oz (10 ml) lemonade mix syrup (Monin)
- BEER: Session IPA
- A few pieces of pineapple (or 1 fl oz [30 ml] juice)
- 1 apple (or 1 fl oz [30 ml] juice)
- 1 wedge of grilled grapefruit
- Ice

IN THE SHAKER

1 - Mash all the fruit pieces in a shaker and add all the ingredients except the beer and garnish.

2 - Fill shaker with ice and shake.

3 - Serve over ice, double filtered.

4 - Top with beer and stir.

5 - Garnish: a wedge of grilled grapefruit.

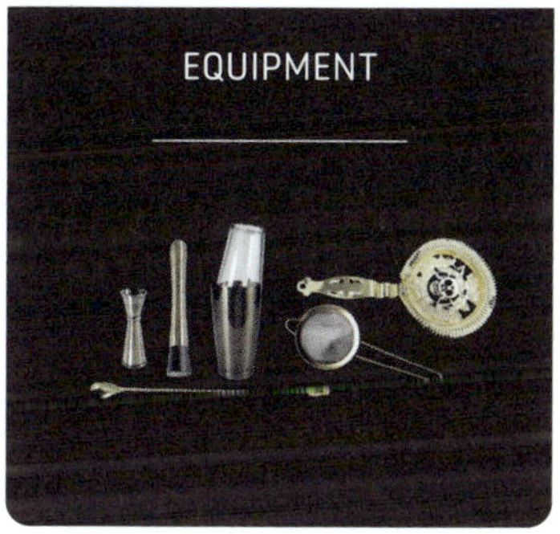

JUNGLE BIRD

GLASS TYPE: OLD FASHIONED

INGREDIENTS:

- 1⅓ fl oz (40 ml) dark rum XO (Duppy Share)
- 1 fl oz (30 ml) Campari
- A few pineapple pieces (or 2 fl oz [60 ml] juice)
- ⅓ fl oz (10 ml) lemon juice
- ⅔ fl oz (20 ml) blood orange syrup (Monin)
- BEER: American IPA
- Ice

IN THE SHAKER

1 – Mash a few pineapple chunks in a shaker, then add all the ingredients except the beer.

2 – Fill shaker with ice and shake.

3 – Serve over ice, double filtered.

4 – Top with beer and stir.

5 – Garnish: a pineapple leaf.

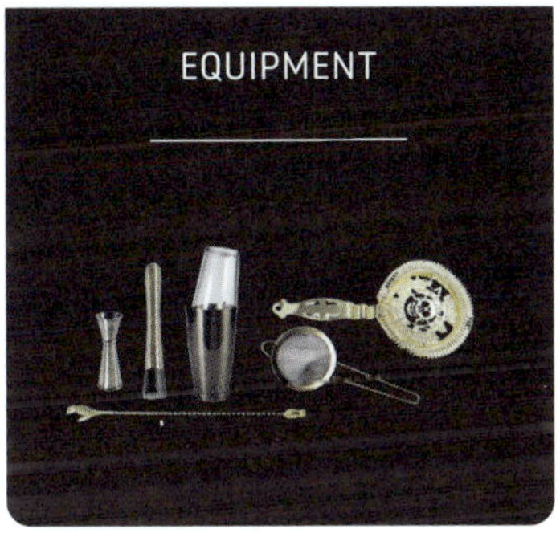

EMERALD

GLASS TYPE: LARGE COUPE

INGREDIENTS:

- 1⅓ fl oz (40 ml) dark rum 8 years (Camikara)
- 1 fl oz (30 ml) Koskenkorva ginger liqueur
- ½ fl oz (15 ml) blue curaçao (Giffard)
- ⅓ fl oz (10 ml) squeezed lemon juice
- A few pieces of pineapple (or 3⅓ fl oz [100 ml] juice)
- BEER: American IPA
- Ice

IN THE SHAKER

1 – Reserving some for the garnish, mash the pineapple chunks in a shaker and pour in all the ingredients except the beer.

2 – Fill shaker with ice and shake.

3 – Serve over ice, double filtered.

4 – Top with beer and stir.

5 – Garnish: ½ slice pineapple.

SWEET SURPRISE

GLASS TYPE: TASTING

INGREDIENTS:

- 1⅓ fl oz (40 ml) Edmond gin
- ⅓ fl oz (10 ml) green banana syrup (Monin)
- 1 dash of chocolate bitters (Fee Brothers)
- BEER: mango Pale Ale
- 1 egg white
- 1 banana chip
- Dried flowers

IN THE SHAKER

1 – Pour all the ingredients except the beer and garnish into a shaker and do an initial shake.

2 – Fill with ice, then shake it again.

3 – Serve over ice, double filtered.

4 – Top with beer and stir.

5 – Garnish: banana chip and dried flowers.

VIRGIN LIMINO

EQUIPMENT

GLASS TYPE: LARGE COUPE

INGREDIENTS:

- 1⅓ fl oz (40 ml) alcohol-free limoncello
- BEER: Alcohol-free Pale Ale with grapefruit and guava, or with tropical fruits
- 2 scoops lime sorbet

IN THE SHAKER

1 – Place the glass and lime in the freezer.

2 – Grate lime zest into the bottom of the glass, reserving some for the garnish.

3 – Add the sorbet and limoncello.

4 – Top with beer.

5 – Garnish: lime zest.

GOLDEN WHISKY SOUR

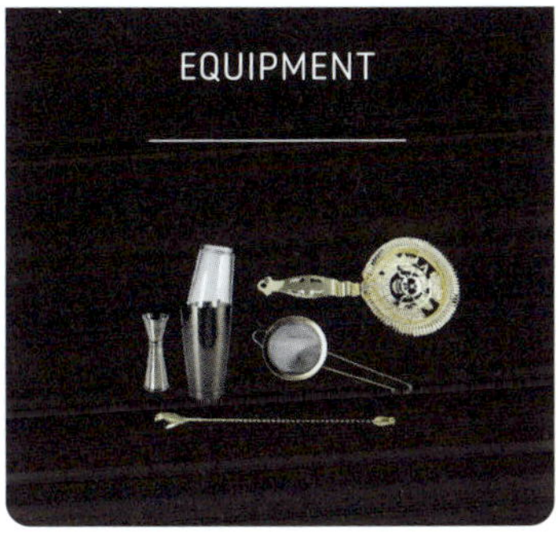

GLASS TYPE: OLD FASHIONED

INGREDIENTS:

- 1⅓ fl oz (40 ml) whisky 36 months (Belgian Howl)
- ⅔ fl oz (20 ml) lemon juice
- ⅔ fl oz (20 ml) beer syrup
- BEER: New Zealand IPA (CR/AK Brewery)
- 1 egg white
- Lemon peel
- 1 Amarena cherry
- Ice

IN THE SHAKER

1 – Make a cold syrup with the beer.

2 – Pour all the ingredients except the beer and garnish into the shaker and do an initial dry shake.

3 – Fill the shaker with ice and shake it again.

4 – Serve over ice, double filtered.

5 – Top with beer and stir.

6 – Garnish: lemon peel and an Amarena cherry.

LAGER

This category is quite broad. Low-fermentation beers are relatively accessible, mellow, not very aromatic, malty, and hoppy. They either have a pronounced bitterness or no strong flavors, are often dry, with a beautiful clarity, well-balanced, and very fizzy. Served cold, they are refreshing and thirst-quenching. Here are some lager-based cocktails.

MELODY

GLASS TYPE: COUPE

INGREDIENTS:

- 1⅓ fl oz (40 ml) single malt whisky (Taisteal)
- 1 fl oz (30 ml) elderflower liqueur (Ellenor)
- ⅔ fl oz (20 ml) maple and spice syrup (Monin)
- A few strawberries (or 1 fl oz [30 ml] juice)
- ⅔ fl oz (20 ml) lemon juice
- 1 dash rhubarb bitters (Fee Brothers)
- BEER: 1885 Lager (Tennent's Brewery)
- 1 egg white
- Ice

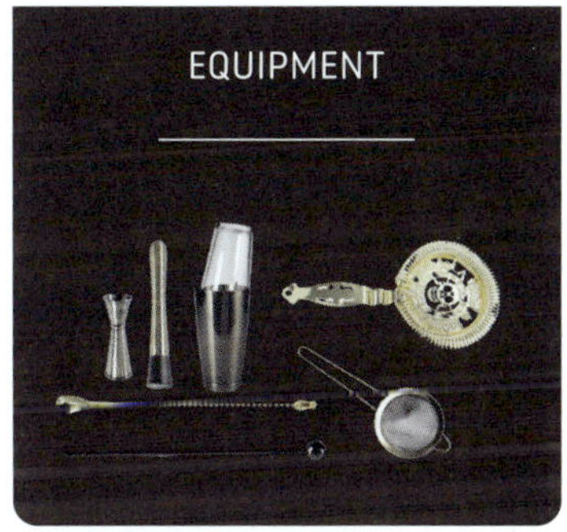

IN THE SHAKER

1 – Reserving some for the garnish, mash a few strawberries in a shaker, pour in all the ingredients except the beer and do an initial dry shake.

2 – Fill with ice, then shake it again.

3 – Serve through a double strainer.

4 – Top with beer and stir.

5 – Garnish: a strawberry skewer.

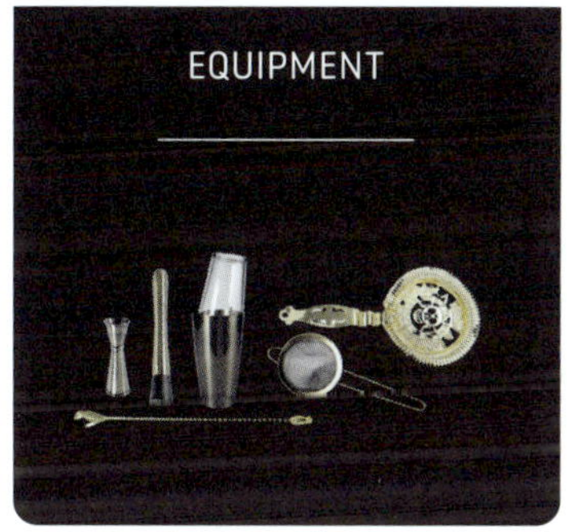

DRAGARITA

GLASS TYPE: OLD FASHIONED

INGREDIENTS:

- 1⅓ fl oz (40 ml) Espadín mezcal (Noble Coyote)
- ⅔ fl oz (20 ml) triple sec Dry Curaçao (Maison Ferrand)
- 1 fl oz (30 ml) lime juice
- A few pieces of red dragonfruit (or 1⅓ fl oz [40 ml] juice)
- ½ fl oz (15 ml) agave syrup (Monin)
- BEER: a dry, slightly bitter International Pale Lager style beer
- 1 pinch pink salt
- 1 slice of lime
- Ice

IN THE SHAKER

1 – Reserving some for the garnish, mash a few pieces of red dragonfruit in a shaker, then pour in all the ingredients except the beer and garnishes.

2 – Fill shaker with ice and shake.

3 – Serve through a double strainer.

4 – Top with beer and stir.

5 – Garnish: a slice of red dragonfruit and a slice of lime.

EQUIPMENT

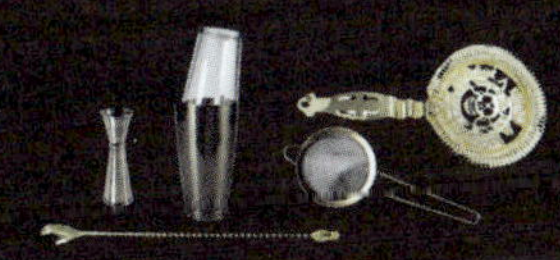

BLUE CANARY

GLASS TYPE: FLUTE

INGREDIENTS:

- 1⅓ fl oz (40 ml) Old Tom gin (Langley's)
- ⅔ fl oz (20 ml) blue curaçao liqueur (Giffard)
- ¾ fl oz (25 ml) lemon juice
- ¾ fl oz (25 ml) coconut milk
- BEER: a lager-style beer with citrus notes
- 1 egg white
- Canary Islands nasturtiums
- A little cane sugar syrup
- Ice

IN THE SHAKER

1 – Rim one side of the glass with cane sugar syrup and Canary Island nasturtiums.

2 – Pour all the ingredients into the shaker, except the beer, and do an initial dry shake.

3 – Fill with ice, shake it again.

4 – Serve through a double strainer.

5 – Top with beer and stir.

6 – Garnish: rim with Canary Island nasturtiums.

STOUTS AND PORTER

These two Anglo-Saxon styles share a common origin but have evolved to become distinct from each other in terms of taste profile and appearance. At times low in alcohol, dark in color and made from brown malt, they offer notes of roasted malt, including tones of chocolate, cocoa, coffee, caramel, toast, licorice, molasses, and even tar. Here are some cocktails featuring these styles of beer.

EQUIPMENT

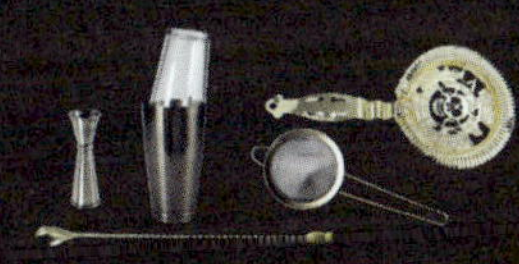

PORTEFAIX

GLASS TYPE: BOSTON

INGREDIENTS:

- ⅓ fl oz (10 ml) sugar syrup
- ⅓ fl oz (10 ml) Elo Amo tequila
- ⅓ fl oz (10 ml) Roku gin
- ⅓ fl oz (10 ml) Haku vodka
- ⅓ fl oz (10 ml) dark rum R74 (Ronner)
- ⅓ fl oz (10 ml) triple sec (Giffard)
- ⅓ fl oz (10 ml) lime juice
- BEER: English Porter
- Ice
- 1 slice dried lime
- A pansy

IN THE SHAKER

1 – Pour all ingredients into the shaker, except the beer and garnishes.

2 – Fill shaker with ice and shake.

3 – Serve through a double strainer.

4 – Top with beer and stir.

5 – Garnish: a slice of dried lime and a pansy.

EQUIPMENT

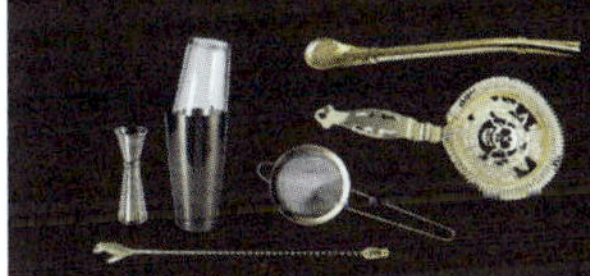

BOX OFFICE

GLASS TYPE: OLD FASHIONED

INGREDIENTS:

- 1 fl oz (30 ml) Spiced dark rum (Gun's Bell)
- ⅓ fl oz (10 ml) Mozart dark chocolate liqueur
- ⅓ fl oz (10 ml) salted caramel syrup (Monin)
- 1 passion fruit (or ⅔ fl oz [20 ml] juice)
- BEER: Imperial Stout
- Chocolate topping
- Popcorn
- Ice

IN THE SHAKER

1 – Pour all ingredients into the shaker, except the beer and garnishes.

2 – Fill shaker with ice and shake.

3 – Serve over ice, double filtered.

4 – Top with beer and stir.

5 – Place the glass inside a popcorn box, and add a straw.

6 – Garnish: chocolate topping, popcorn.

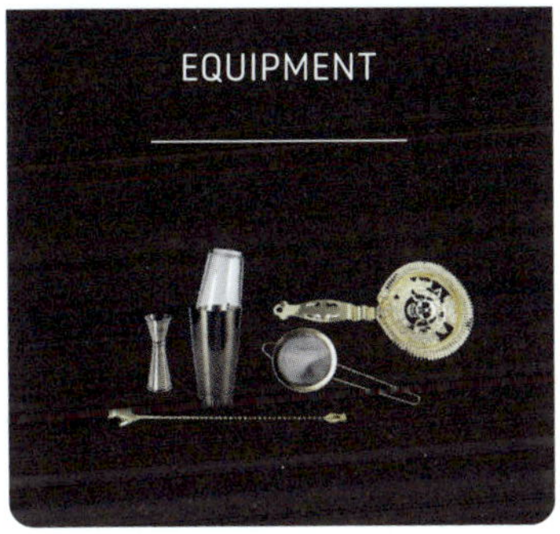

DARK AMARETTO SOUR

GLASS TYPE: OLD FASHIONED

INGREDIENTS:

- 1⅓ fl oz (40 ml) brown amaretto (Adriatico)
- ⅔ fl oz (20 ml) lemon juice
- 1 tsp cane syrup (Monin)
- BEER: Must Kuld Chai Latte (Pohjala Brewery)
- ½ slice candied orange
- 1 raspberry
- Ice

IN THE SHAKER

1 – Pour all ingredients into the shaker, except the beer and garnishes.

2 – Fill shaker with ice and shake.

3 – Serve over ice, double filtered.

4 – Top with beer and stir.

5 – Garnish: ½ slice candied orange and a raspberry.

CHERRY MOCHA

GLASS TYPE: OLD FASHIONED

INGREDIENTS:

- 1 fl oz (30 ml) coffee liqueur (Kahlua)
- ⅔ fl oz (20 ml) cherry liqueur (Vedrenne)
- ⅓ fl oz (10 ml) amaretto liqueur (Giffard)
- BEER: Milk Stout (Black Sheep Brewery)
- Ice
- Chocolate topping
- Chocolate sprinkles
- Maraschino cherries
- Mint leaves

IN THE SHAKER

1 – Rim the glass with chocolate topping and sprinkles.

2 – Pour all the ingredients into the shaker, except the beer and garnishes.

3 – Fill shaker with ice and shake.

4 – Serve over ice, double filtered.

5 – Top with beer and stir.

6 – Garnish: chocolate topping, maraschino cherry skewer and mint leaves.

EQUIPMENT

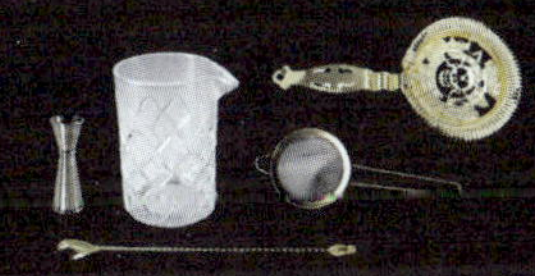

CHUPA CABRA

GLASS TYPE: COUPE

INGREDIENTS:

- 1⅓ fl oz (40 ml) blue agave spirit
- 1⅓ fl oz (40 ml) La Capricieuse (goat's milk liqueur with speculoos flavor)
- ⅓ fl oz (10 ml) whisky liqueur (Shanky's Whip)
- BEER: English Porter
- Speculoos
- Ice

IN A MIXING GLASS

1 – Rim the glass with whisky liqueur and crumbled speculoos.

2 – Pour all ingredients except beer into mixing glass, fill with ice and stir.

3 – Serve through a double strainer.

4 – Top with beer and stir.

5 – Garnish: Speculoos sprinkles.

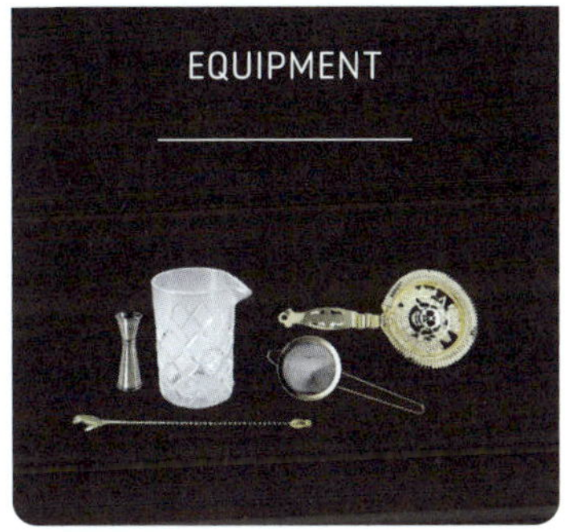

GOLDEN BARI'STOUT

GLASS TYPE: TASTING

INGREDIENTS:

- 1 fl oz (30 ml) Straight Corn whisky (Bowsaw)
- ⅔ fl oz (20 ml) coffee liqueur (Brunette)
- ⅓ fl oz (10 ml) speculoos syrup (Monin)
- 1 cold espresso
- BEER: Imperial Stout
- Chocolate sprinkles and shavings
- 1 maraschino cherry
- Ice

IN A MIXING GLASS

1 – Rim the glass with the syrup, chocolate sprinkles and shavings.

2 – Pour all the ingredients into the mixing glass, except the beer and maraschino cherry.

3 – Fill with ice and stir.

4 – Serve and top with beer, stirring.

5 – Garnish: chocolate sprinkles and shavings rim, maraschino cherry.

ACKNOWLEDGMENTS

Thanks to the participating breweries: Brasseurs Cueilleurs; Brasseurs; Brasserie 1989; Brasserie Azimut; Brasserie Billd; Brasserie Black Pig; Brasserie Bon Poison; Brasserie Brique House; Brasserie de l'Apocalypse; Brasserie De Sully; Brasserie De Troch; Brasserie Delabonne; Brasserie Dunoise; Brasserie Effet Papillon; Brasserie Fauve; Brasserie Grand Duc; Brasserie Grand Paris; Brasserie Jjap; Brasserie Jukebox; Brasserie L'Etuverie; Brasserie La Goutte d'Or; Brasserie La Mine; Brasserie La Parisienne; Brasserie La Plaine; Brasserie LaTruite; Brasserie Le Duff; Brasserie Les Deux Amants; Brasserie Les Intenables; Brasserie Malternative; Brasserie Maltolab; Brasserie Méduz; Brasserie Mogwaï; Brasserie Nemeto; Brasserie Nuka; Brasserie Old Tribe; Brasserie Ouch Nanon; Brasserie Pietra; Brasserie Ragnar; Brasserie Respekt; Brasserie Spore; Brasserie Tête Haute; Brasserie Vetra; Brasserie White Frontier; Brasserie Zoumaï.

Huge thanks to Victor Topart, who created the cocktails on pages 12, 17, 21, 23, 49, 62, 71, 79, 81, 86, 92, 108, 159, 163, 165, 167, 169, 171, 173, 177, 185, 225, 235, 237, 239, 251, 253, 265, 289, 297, & 301. Thanks also to Massin Publishing House. Infinite gratitude to my partner Élodie for her drawings, but above all for her patience and unwavering support during the difficult times (and there were a few). A big thank you to Romeu Martins, the creator of the cocktails on pages 22, 39, 41, 43, 55, 58, 63, 66, 69, 74, 77, 89, 90, 94, 96, 100, 104, 106, 110, 181, 183, 185, 187, 189, 197, 199, 201, 203, 219, 223, 229, 231, 233, 241, 249, 257, 259, 263, 267, 271, 273, 275, 277, 281, 283, 291, & 295. Special thanks to Arc International, Chef & Sommelier, Arcoroc. The cocktails on the following pages were served in their stunning glassware: 16, 41, 79, 81, 86, 92, 94, 102, 159, 161, 167, 185, 193, 197, 205, 211, 217, 225, 233, 237, 241, 243, 251, 253, 255, 269, 271, 273, 283, 285, 287, 289, 293, 295, 297, 301, & 303. Many thanks to Baptiste Vassy/www.lebreuvage.fr. Thanks to photographer Pierre-Michel Delessert for the images in this book. Also thanks to: Les Fleuridées Montreux; Laurence Marot; Carole Nicolas Idées en Forme; Carlos Bolis; Nicolas Bonnet All Beer & Co. And thanks to all the teams behind my wonderful sponsors: Alambics du Coq, Aligro, Amstein, Archibald, Audemus Spirits, Bacanha, BBC Spirits, Bigallet, Black Pig, Bordeaux Distilling Co., Brasseurs BU Unis, Cakelicious, Calvados Roger Groult, Casadeltequila, CBH, Dartigalongue, Des Lis Chocolate, Diva Domaines & Distilleries, Dugas, Distillerie Escagnan, L'Explorateur du Goût Free Spirits Distribution, Giffard, Gin O'Clock, Gueule de Joie, Hedon Distribution, La Capricieuse, La Petite Cave du Chablais, Lateltin, Brasserie Artisanale La Fruite, Le Cercle, Maison Ferrand, Maison Mairot, Marché Cuendet, Monbrun, Mon Drink, Monin, Notion Drinks, Ouche Nanon, Respekt, Roner, Société des Alcools à Papa, Terroirs Distillers, Tessendier & Fils, UCVF and Warenghem.

INDEX OF COCKTAILS

Abyss Candy 189
Adam & Eve 205
Ai Ai Ai! 249
Apocalypse Paradise 22
Archduchess 49
Bahia Samba 239
Basil Instinct 223
Beer Porn Martini 225
Beerini 86
Billy Dawson Punch 19
Black Sea Whisper 89
Blue Canary 295
Blue Velvet 185
Box Office 299
Brambles 269
Candy Red Romance 104
Carnival 259
Celebration 279
Celtic Pear Shandy 87
Charlene Sour 187
Cheeky 265
Cherry Mocha 303
Cherry on Top 159
Chupa Cabra 305
Cigarita 23
Citrus Twist 79
Coppery Sunset 183
Crème Brûlée 243
Dandy War'ale 63
Dark Amaretto Sour 301
Dark Mule 247
Dragarita 293
Emerald 283
Espresso Martini Swing 62
Fiery Belle Époque 5
Forest Serenity 98
Fresh Nog'n'ale 55
Garden Fresh 94
Garden of Eden 237
Golden Bari'stout 307
Golden Whisky Sour 289
Good Fortune 235
Greek Side 177
Green Bermud'ale Devil 207
Green Diosa 219
Grog 58
Hazy Hype Old Fashioned 74
Harmony 241
Imperial 277
Infinito 275
Juicy Jungle 193
Jungle Bird 281
Kiwi Kicker 83
Lucky Samurai 215
Lychee Lullaby 263
Mai Tai Tropical Sour 173
Malt Attack 163
Margote 161
Mary's Hot Dog 92
Matcha Margarita Sour 102
Meeting 261
Melody 291
Mexican D'artagnan Mule 181
Millionaire 37 203
Mint Chocobeet Rum 213
Mint Hop Julep 257
Misty Sea Around The Island 217
Moscow Mule 13
Nautic'ale 211
Nerii Treasure 245
New Horse's Neck 12
N'imp'chimp 53
Old Fashioned Chocopeanut 253
Old Fashioned Cozy Retreat 100
Old Pal 39
Pamplo-Mango 66
Passionately 273
Pineapple Cove 179
Pink Badass 167
Pink Refresher 221
Polar Paloma 267
Portefaix 297
Porto Back Flip 69
Provencial 96
Pump It Up 175
Purity 25
Purple in Love 191
Raspberry Bouquet 85
Red Reflection 209
Rosy Riviera 271
Rustic Mule 231
Sazerac Spirit 17
Serenade 233
Sidecar in Hollywood 21
Smoked Old Fashioned Pickle Sweet & Sour 11
Southern Vegetable Garden 108
Sour Poppino 195
Summer Splash 227
Sunburn 165
Sweet Surprise 285
Tanguy Chill 41
The Beer Lebowski 71
The Insolent 77
Thirsty Dandy 251
To My Love 197
Tropic Colada Sour 169
Tropical Crush 255
Tropicool 199
Ulysses 41 229
Unusual Purl 16
Valhall'ale Nog 81
Velvet Coffee 106
Virgin Limino 287
Voodoo Carnival 171
White Sea Whisper 90
Wo Pink 201
Yellow Pisco Sour 43

ABOUT THE AUTHOR

Cyril Hubert is a Switzerland-based beerologist and beer sommelier. With a background in traditional and gastronomic catering, he specializes in beerology. He organizes and leads introductory tasting workshops, consults for brewers and restaurateurs, and is a member of the jury of numerous international competitions.

cyrilhubertbierologue
les-degustateurs.com